# AMERICAN VICTORIAN ARCHITECTURE

## A SURVEY OF THE 70's AND 80's IN CONTEMPORARY PHOTOGRAPHS

With a New Introduction by
### ARNOLD LEWIS
Professor of Art History, The College of Wooster

and Notes on the Plates by
### KEITH MORGAN

Dover Publications, Inc., New York

Published in Canada by General Publishing Company, Ltd., 30 Lesmill Road, Don Mills, Toronto, Ontario.
Published in the United Kingdom by Constable and Company, Ltd., 10 Orange Street, London WC 2.

This Dover edition, first published in 1975, is an unabridged republication of the work originally titled *L'Architecture Américaine* and published by André, Daly fils Cie, Paris, in 1886. A new Introduction by Arnold Lewis and Notes by Keith Morgan (pp. 139-152) have been prepared specially for this edition. The publisher would like to thank the Architektursammlung, Technische Universität, Munich, for lending the only known extant copy of *L'Architecture Américaine* for reproduction. Without their cooperation this volume could not have been published.

*International Standard Book Number: 0–486–23177–1*
*Library of Congress Catalog Card Number: 73–92261*

Manufactured in the United States of America
Dover Publications, Inc.
180 Varick Street
New York, N.Y. 10014

# CONTENTS

# LIST OF PLATES

# INTRODUCTION

## FRENCH, BRITISH, AND GERMAN CRITICISM BEFORE 1886

THE PUBLICATION of *L'Architecture Américaine* early in 1886 provided French architects with a remarkably thorough and perceptive photographic anthology of recent buildings in the United States. Why the firm of André, Daly fils et C$^{ie}$ issued this pictorial study, however, is puzzling because the architects in Paris had largely ignored the activities of the profession across the Atlantic. They had written only occasionally about American work, and, in virtually every instance, had passed judgments without making the ocean voyage. César Daly (1811–1893)—architect, author, editor, archaeologist, member of numerous national societies of architects, Chevalier of the Legion of Honor and recipient of the 1892 Gold Medal of the Royal Institute of British Architects (R.I.B.A.)—had been for thirty years a rare foreign voice of encouragement for the American designers, yet even his support had been vague and sporadic. He had expected to find buildings radiating a "go-ahead spirit" free from the "imperious tyranny of tradition" when he visited New York in 1856.[1] Disappointed by the architecture he saw, he rationalized that such an art could not be fashioned overnight and, furthermore, the United States was indeed influenced by its European heritage. Decades later, acting like a sage whose wisdom and perspective permitted him to see both the promise and the wrong turns of an apprentice, Daly advised the Americans to relax and let art work its magic: "Re-establish the natural harmony of things, after science and business, art; after work, recreation or rest; after calling on the positive activity of reasoning, let the dreaming imagination and the heart's feelings soar; after the true and the utilitarian, invoke the beautiful; and well-being will come abundantly to you, with health of body and soul."[2] Daly's final comment on the United States in 1886, in his own *Revue Générale de l'Architecture et Travaux Publics*, implied that if he were to visit New York City then he would see architecture which would measure up to his earlier expectations. The country and its builders were learning at an unprecedented pace, he informed his readers. The American used European traditions like "an orange which he squeezes and sucks dry before tossing away the peel."[3]

Most of Daly's friends would have been unconcerned about his judgments; a few might have objected to them. In the wake of the Philadelphia Centennial in 1876, French periodicals had published a few curt references, often to cite a quantitatively impressive fact or the latest Yankee sensation or gaucherie. No doubt the need to lend symmetry to the column layout on a page often proved a more compelling motive for writing than genuine curiosity. The only extensive survey of contemporary work was written for the *Revue Générale* in 1877 by Camille-Marie Piton (1842–?), a Parisian architect who had attended the Philadelphia Exposition.[4] He discovered weaknesses inside and outside of the exposition grounds: the contractor dominated the architect; the country had no national school of design, an institution which would have curbed aberrations created under the pretext of independent thinking; builders placed too high a value on experimentation; and the public tolerated artistic deceit. In agreement with the majority of French critics prior to the mid eighties, Piton argued that fine art was unattainable for a Western nation until the conditions were right. In his view, art was the culmination of a centuries-long process similar to physical maturation. It could only be achieved when a nation had resolved the practical problems of earning its living and could enjoy leisure time to meditate. The United States, far from this stage of contemplative detachment, was experiencing the "engineering" or "utilitarian" phase of its development. For this reason, try as the Americans might, they would be unable—according to Piton—to create art of a quality expected of European countries such as France in which the prerequisites of age, stability, and factors encouraging contemplation existed. American designers annoyed the French because they seemed either unable to understand or unwilling to respect the truth of this biological analogy. Before their country was thoroughly settled, before their cities had ceased to grow disruptively, before their clients were willing to stop their incessant dollar hunting to think of higher values, these confident but naive men believed they could produce masterpieces. But neither cockiness nor determination nor chance would hurry the process. Neither would experimentation, simplification, short-cuts, substitutions, or new technology hasten the day when American architecture became respectable. To the contrary, by leaping over essential steps, they were prolonging that moment.

Occasionally, a French writer commended some aspect of architecture in the United States. For example, an article in the *Encyclopédie d'Architecture*, reviewing the contributions of nineteenth-century expositions, praised the Centennial for its beautiful setting and pervasive concern for comfort.[5] Paul Planat (1839–1911), the founder of both *La Semaine des Constructeurs* and *La Construction Moderne*, as well as editor of the multi-volume *L'Encyclopédie de L'Architecture et de la Construction*, remarked in 1877 that American schools were hygienic and comfortable and revealed the willingness of citizens to spend money to obtain satisfactory results.[6] The only type of building which attracted any enthusiastic comment was the detached, private house. Between 1876 and 1885 the *Gazette des Architectes et du Bâtiment* published illustrations of fourteen houses, calling specific attention to their unclassical, asymmetrical elevations. This was the same aspect which appealed to Jean Boussard (1844–1923), the editor of *Le Moniteur des Architectes*, when he quizzically examined in 1885 a small, rural house designed by Cass Gilbert.[7] But these were clearly exceptions to the general attitude

which held that the criteria that really mattered—harmony of parts, refined proportions, discreet and scholarly ornament—were not the distinguishing marks of American design. The majority would have agreed with Piton: despite the great progress of the United States, art in general, and architecture in particular, left much to be desired.[8]

If these photographs of contemporary architecture in the United States had been published in London or in Berlin instead of Paris, the event would have been somewhat less surprising. During the early eighties the relationship between the *American Architect*, the professional journal most respected abroad, and journals in Great Britain was more active. Yet, their exchanges were often childish—"[Ventilation] is also a matter of every-day practice in England, though the assumption appears to be that ventilating a building here [in Britain] is a most curious scientific and withal uncertain sort of proceeding such as attracts a sort of 'wild-west-show' interest"[9]—, revealing the self-confidence of the American editors and the readily flammable responses of their English counterparts. Also, the criticism by the British was colored by paternalistic sniping at Brother Jonathan. Nevertheless, they had a better idea of what was happening architecturally in the United States than did the French. Unlike the French, they read the American journals and often reprinted articles from them. Many of the British had crossed the ocean; the French had not.

The catalyst of serious British criticism was the Godwin Bursary, a grant established in 1881 and administered by the R.I.B.A. to encourage young architects to study aspects of construction, sanitation, and ventilation in Europe or North America. The first recipient of the award, John Arthur Gale (d. 1928), selected the United States. Returning from a three-month tour in 1882, he spoke favorably at the December meeting of the membership about the work he had seen. The comments which followed his address indicated that opinion on the subject was heated and mixed. President Ewan Christian concluded the discussion by stating that the "go-a-headness" there meant the adoption of inventions before they were perfected, something the British unfortunately would not do.[10] Gale's findings provoked a series of defensive and opinionated editorials in the *Architect*, the *Building News* and the *Builder* until 1884.[11] John B. Gass (1855–1939) another Bursary winner, chose the United States in 1885. In his report he praised not only the practical but also the artistic achievements of the buildings he had seen:

> The best specimens of it are scholarly and refined in detail, but adhere less slavishly to precedent than European work, and new combinations, dictated by and growing out of the necessities of the building, are introduced. Selecting a style in which to work, an American architect is less fettered by tradition than his European brethren, and though in no way violating its character, often employs it in a new and original manner, and with truer regard to its principles. His work is accordingly more living and interesting, less the production of a dry-as-dust archaeology,

and more in accordance with the true principles of all great architecture.[12]

In March of 1886 at the Institute, Gass arranged the first European exhibition of the latest American work. Containing approximately 130 drawings and photographs, the exhibition emphasized the architecture of Henry Richardson, Richard M. Hunt, H. J. Hardenbergh, Peabody and Stearns, Adler and Sullivan, Burnham and Root, McKim, Mead, and White, George Post, Addison Hutton, and T. P. Chandler.

This exhibition and these accounts by returning Bursary winners influenced the thinking of those who formed the nucleus of the British profession. After these events it was more difficult to reject categorically the efforts of the Americans; as the critics of the seventies had done, or even to pass on a derogatory joke about their strange and inapplicable practices. Yet many members of the profession in Britain were skeptical. American work might be practical, but artistic? Older architects had spent years— even decades—collecting stories to illustrate that the fine arts did not prosper in this raw land. They could hardly be expected to endorse without suspicion the conclusions which Gale and Gass had reached. Collectively, the British probably regarded the American development uneasily in the mid eighties, unsure of how much of it was believable and applicable to their own architecture. Robert Kerr (1823–1904) expressed this uncertainty well in 1885 when he was professor of the arts of construction at Kings College, London. Generalizing about the leading nations of architecture, he called the English practical and sentimental, the French supreme in matters of art, the Germans inartistic and lacking in esprit, the Italians traditionalists, and the Americans youthful but eager to take Europe's place when she faltered. For the British in 1885, the Americans were waiting in the wings, not yet known members of the company but keen to enter the play in the next act.[13]

Despite their skepticism, the British were better informed than were the French prior to 1886, when *L'Architecture Américaine* appeared. Accordingly, we might have expected such a set of elegant photographs to be published first in London. But if they had been, the news would have bowled over the praise-hungry editors of the *American Architect* who were constantly culling the foreign press for words about the United States. Throughout this decade these editors complained about the poor press they thought American work received in England. "We are quite accustomed to the attitudes of English critics—both those who come to see for themselves, and those who do not think it worthwhile to do even that . . ."[14] If we take into account the *American Architect's* assessment of British thinking and Robert Kerr's honor roll of nations, we must conclude that 1886 was hardly the moment for any British publisher to risk a major publication on the subject of American architecture.

Germany was the only other European country in which architects had some idea of what was happening in the United States. Before 1884 few articles on the subject appeared in German periodicals; however, the tone and thrust of this criticism differed from that in Britain and France. Unlike the critics of these countries, German writers seldom pointed out the artistic weaknesses of the buildings they described. Instead, they emphasized methodology and the relationship between the architect and engineer in the United States. Furthermore, their comments were relatively free from belittling comparisons or pompous advice, possibly because they saw a parallel between Germany, since its unification in 1871 the youngest nation of Europe, and America, the adolescent giant of the New World.

The German government sent Franz Lange (1830–1916), an engineer who had studied at the Bauakademie in Berlin, to Washington, D.C. in 1882 to serve as technical attaché at the German Embassy. His responsibility was to study new developments in engineering and architecture and to keep the ministry in Berlin informed about these developments. In August 1884 he addressed the prestigious assembly of the Verband deutscher Architekten und Ingenieure held in Stuttgart, discussing for the first time before a German audience the practice and results he had observed in the United States. His role in Germany in 1884 was similar to Gale's in England in 1882, but his report—without focus, unclear, and overgeneralized— was inferior.[15] Lange was replaced in Washington by Karl Hinckeldeyn (1847–1927) who served in the United States until 1887. Formerly on the staff of the *Centralblatt der Bauverwaltung*, he was the first trained architect to act as technical attaché at German embassies in London, Paris, and Washington. His first judgments were decisive and negative. He called the Washington Monument purposeless, the buildings of the 1884–1885 New Orleans Exposition bare and unfinished, and houses designed in the Queen Anne mode exaggerations of reasonable plans. In addition, he told the Chicago architects they were foolish and arrogant to think their new office buildings attractive and condemned the profession in New York for perpetuating an ineffective, corruption-susceptible building code.[16] These were his published views when *L'Architecture Américaine* appeared. At that moment, no European critic was more knowledgeable about building in the United States. He was probably stunned to learn that some Parisian firm thought there would be a market for such a title. Gradually Hinckeldeyn altered his earlier conclusions. These reassessments trickled out slowly in articles during the late eighties and early nineties, but he did not venture a major publication himself until 1897, when he wrote a short but perceptive introduction to one hundred photographs of contemporary architecture in the United States which was entitled *Neubauten in Nordamerika*.[17]

To summarize, European architects and critics were curious but not knowledgeable about architectural developments in the United States at the beginning of 1886. During the first half of the 1880s several young British architects had visited the country and reported their findings to the R.I.B.A. Although the German government sent representatives to Washington to study American engineering and architecture, their first reports were not complimentary. A few French critics praised this work, but these men had reached their conclusions on French soil with the aid of illustrations, primarily from the *American Architect*.

## THE PUBLICATION AND IMPACT OF *L'ARCHITECTURE AMÉRICAINE*

Why then was *L'Architecture Américaine* published at all? The question cannot be answered neatly. Not the result of popular demand, the project was probably the inspiration of one of the few French architects who had followed the activities of the American profession. André, Daly fils et C[ie] issued the three albums. André was probably Adolphe André, a member of the staff of the *Revue Générale* since 1875. At the journal he would have met the two sons of César Daly, Marcel (1860–?) and Raymond (1862–?). There is no evidence that André wrote about the United States, and Raymond signed only one article in the late nineteenth century, an obituary of Richard Morris Hunt.[18] Marcel, however, published a series of favorable studies between 1886 and 1892.[19]

His first study, January 9, 1886, noted the improvement in American work in the previous three decades; his second, June 12, 1886, characterized this architecture as "youthful" and "full of suggestions." In the latter, Marcel quoted his father's tributes which had appeared earlier that year in "Maisons américaines" in the *Revue Générale* and then urged his readers who wanted more evidence to purchase *L'Architecture Américaine*. Of the three members of the firm, he was the most outspoken and consistent defender of American practice, and the one most likely to have pushed the project. On the other hand, his father may have been involved; he may have procured or commissioned the photographs and then passed them on to his sons. Evidence for this possibility comes from his article, "Maisons américaines," a footnote to which announced, "The office of André, Daly fils et C[ie] is presently publishing three reasonably priced albums of photographs showing the most recent buildings in the United States of North America." His article contained engravings of six town houses prepared from photographs attributed to a Mr. A. Levy. Normally, when the French wanted illustrations of American buildings, they took them from American journals; for example, Marcel Daly lifted the illustrations for his June 1886 article from the *Sanitary Engineer* and the *American Architect*. However, the engravings in "Maisons américaines" appear to have been made from photographs similar to those included in volume two of *L'Architecture Américaine*. Conceivably, then, César Daly appropriated plates which had been prepared for the photographic survey but which were not included among the published pictures. Thus, he may have had a hand in planning the project, and Levy may have been the photographer for some or all of the 120 plates.

Not only do those who commissioned the project and photographed the buildings remain obscure, it is also difficult to gauge accurately its reception among European architects. André, Daly fils et C[ie] apparently did not lose money on the title; yet, other indicators suggest that the impact of these albums on Paris, London, and Berlin was inconsequential. Although we do not know the cost of the three sets or how many were printed or sold, we might suppose that the firm at least broke even because it announced a second photographic study, *Villas Américaines*, two years later. Regrettably, information about the contents and reception of this work is even scarcer. Since no copy has been located, we might assume that it was planned and announced but never published, the fate, apparently, of at least two late nineteenth-century European studies of American work.[20] But both *La Semaine des Constructeurs* and the *American Architect* acknowledged it, the latter observing, "The new firm of architectural book publishers in Paris, Messrs. André, Daly and C[ie], have just published a book on 'Villas Américaines,' in which the work of the profession here seems to be fairly presented. . . ."[21] Actually, the announcement of the second title could mean that there had been no audience for the first, for accompanying the note in *La Semaine* was a plate of a house in Orange, New Jersey, which the editor claimed had been taken from *Villas Américaines*.[22] The house was attributed to a Mr. Dodd—probably Arthur Hooper Dodd. Curiously, the plate was identical to number nine of volume three of *L'Architecture Américaine*, identified in the original table of contents as an anonymously designed house in Orange, New Jersey. Because of this correspondence, *Villas Américaines*, issued in 1888, could be a republication of volume three of *L'Architecture Américaine*. If this were true, it might be argued that the sales of the first project were poor, and to move the stock one set of photographs was retitled and published two years later. Why the third part and not the other two? Because by 1888 the French had chosen the detached, one-family house as the most captivating product of the Yankee designers. In their opinion, public and religious architecture was unsophisticated and commercial buildings coarse and offensive, but the charming "home" was a tribute to family life. If reissued, these photographs would have been less representative of contemporary domestic work in the United States in 1888 than when they originally appeared, but the reception among the French would probably have been more favorable.

In balance, the sales of *L'Architecture Américaine* were probably slower than the firm had anticipated. Though they watched for reactions abroad like hawks, the editors of the *American Architect* failed to review or mention it. French periodicals cited the title a few times, but the press in other European countries did not. Today, copies of the three sets are extremely difficult to locate.[23]

Since the eighties, architectural historians appear to have forgotten it or have been unaware that it was published.

## *L'ARCHITECTURE AMÉRICAINE*'S IMAGE OF AMERICAN ARCHITECTURE

The photographs were divided into three parts according to building types: *Édifices publics et établissements privés*, *Habitations urbaines*, and *Habitations suburbaines*. Despite the absence of any text, the selection of buildings, architects and locations gave a distinctive, if unbalanced, picture of architecture in the United States. Previously, French journals had not reported that commercial buildings were conspicuous features in American cities and were steadily increasing in height. Surprisingly, more than half of the forty plates in the first volume stressed these facts. Among the tall office buildings were several from Chicago—which was also surprising because this was the first time the tall buildings of the city were illustrated abroad. The editors included photographs of Adler and Sullivan's Rothschild Store (I.39), prophetic for its facade of glass, and two by Burnham and Root, the National Bank of Illinois (I.24) and the Insurance Exchange (I.26) precursors of the firm's more famous Rookery Building. They also included the twelve-story Mallers Building by J. J. Flanders (I.25), which, according to Carl Condit,[24] was the highest masonry building in the country when it was completed in 1885. These photographs appeared concurrently with the first plans and illustrations of Chicago's new office buildings published in England,[25] and they anticipated the uneasy European fascination with Chicago, considered in the early nineties the most amazing city of the Western world and reluctantly accepted as an ominous harbinger of the metropolis of the twentieth century. From New York, the editors picked several office buildings which have been appreciated by later architectural historians: two by George B. Post, the Produce Exchange (I.11) and the Mills Building (I.23), and the neatly composed Sloane Carpet Company by W. Wheeler Smith (I.29). They also displayed a doubtful talent for finding buildings undistinguished then or now, such as the three fussy, ecclectic office structures in Baltimore attributed to C. L. Carson (I.33, 34, 35). To their credit, they included an extremely fine photograph of Henry Richardson's Cheney Block in Hartford, Connecticut (I.27), one o the few commercial buildings from the seventies in the collection.

The number of photographs devoted to business buildings in volume one is unexpectedly large. Just as the Academy had prescribed the relative worth of subjects for painters in the eighteenth century, the French profession assumed an unwritten hierarchy of building types in the nineteenth century. Business was crass and business buildings were less edifying than governmental, educa-tional, religious, and cultural architecture. Nevertheless, only 17 of the 120 plates depicted the work of the Americans in these four categories. The selection, however, reveals an understanding of movements in religious and public architecture in the seventies and early eighties which intermingled to form what Europeans around 1890 called the "American style" or the "modern Roman-esque."

The compilers showed their overwhelming preference for the domestic architecture of the United States in the second and third albums. The second contained plates of costly urban mansions, smaller town houses and undistinguished row houses of the larger cities. The third concentrated almost exclusively upon the suburban or resort one-family house. A Frenchman who relied on these plates for his insights into American architecture would conclude that the most splendid urban palaces, identified as *hôtels privés*, existed in New York and Boston. The foremost among them were erected in New York for several members of the Vanderbilt family (II.1–6), the last designed in a sixteenth-century French chateau style by a former student at the École, Richard Morris Hunt. The best examples of row houses could be found in New York and Boston, and those of smaller town houses in the inland cities, especially Chicago. Selections from the third volume were found in watering places like Elberon, New Jersey, and Bar Harbor, Maine, or in residential satellites like Orange, New Jersey and Brookline, Massachusetts. In effect, this set declared that the region between New Jersey and Maine offered the best sampling of picturesque dwellings. The second album celebrated scale, richness, formality and material well-being; the third expressed wealth more modestly and informally. The imposing houses of the cities were brick or masonry; those outside of urban areas frame or combinations of wood and stone. Part two suggested that American architecture was substantial; part three that it was picturesque. Architects included in the third volume—among them, McKim, Mead and White, W. R. Emerson, Peabody and Stearns, Rotch and Tilden, Bruce Price, J. L. Silsbee, and Henry Richardson—are better known today than the architects of the second volume, but even here the perceptive editors picked buildings by Post, Hunt, Peabody and Stearns, Burnham and Root, W. L. B. Jenney, Emerson, and Richardson.

After studying *L'Architecture Américaine*, our hypothetical Frenchman would probably have reached the following conclusions about the profession. Despite the vastness of the country, the leading architects worked in a relatively small area—the northeast section marked by Bar Harbor and Minneapolis in the north and Washington and St. Louis in the south. While these architects designed buildings in many cities and towns, they produced the best urban architecture in New York, Chicago and Boston and the best suburban and country houses in New England. An individual or a firm often accepted commissions in places quite far apart. Judging from the tables of contents, many architects and firms were active. If their importance could be measured by the number of times their buildings were illustrated, the most important were Peabody and Stearns (11), Henry Richardson (9), George B. Post (6), W. R. Emerson (4), Wheelock and Clay (4), Cabot and Chandler (3), Burnham and Root (3), J. L. Silsbee (3), and C. L. Carson (3).

This picture did not conform entirely to the prevailing French image of American work in the mid eighties. In the first place, *L'Architecture Américaine* offered a rich and diversified set of specific examples. To this date the French had seen few engravings of recent architecture in their journals—approximately twenty-five had been published between 1880 and 1886—and American journals, read in London, were not conspicuous in Paris. Nor did the limited number of studies written for French periodicals sharpen their focus. César Daly had been smitten—"Bravo America! Go ahead! Hurrah!"— but beyond generalizing about "a boldness of composition, the daring of conviction, a sense of comfort and interior luxury," he did little to clarify the distant scene. If their understanding was superficial because of insufficient illustrations and sincere but unsystematic analyses, French architects and critics probably had opinions, and strong ones too. Ignorance has seldom deterred conviction. Although they lacked specifics, they learned a great deal about the United States from the accounts of travelers and articles in the popular press. They probably accepted the common assumption that the character of a nation's arts reflects the character of the nation. Without adequate knowledge of American architecture, they may have been influenced by their impressions of the country and its citizens. If this were the case, they would have characterized the art as audacious, experimental, independently created, utilitarian, restless, spacious, prosaic, unscholarly in detail, naively composed, unrefined, extravagant, wasteful, transitory, undeveloped and incomplete. The photographs in *L'Architecture Américaine* would have verified many of these preconceptions. After all, tall office buildings were enormous and coarse, products of a bold, untraditional outlook. Measured against French criteria, several buildings would have seemed unnecessarily primitive for the late nineteenth century, the town houses of the Vanderbilts pretentious and extravagant, the frame houses suggestive of temporary settlement, and the nervous skylines naively designed. On the other hand, they probably would not have expected the excellent materials visible in the photographs, or the solidity expressed by the larger masonry houses, or the esprit of the volumetrically complex houses in wood.

## EUROPEAN CRITICISM IN 1886

If *L'Architecture Américaine* was an untimely publication, presenting a picture of new buildings in the United States not completely in accordance with the stereotypic views of the French, it was also an extremely prophetic anthology in the relationship between French and American architects in the eighties and nineties. Normally, art critics express their first ideas about a new theme in articles; if the theme continues to attract them, they may attempt a book. To illustrate, Samuel Bing wrote *La Culture Artistique en Amérique* in 1895.[26] His lengthy discussion of architecture, focusing mainly on Richardson and his influence in the eighties, came at the end of a decade of lively French interest expressed in periodicals. If Bing's study summarized this interest, *L'Architecture Américaine* anticipated it. It was published at the very moment when architects in France, as well as in Germany and Great Britain, ceased to belittle or ignore the achitecture of the United States and began to regard it as "curiously instructive."[27]

Because it was so sensitive to vibrations abroad and uninhibited about reacting to them, the *American Architect* is an excellent seismograph by which we can gauge this transformation in European thinking. Since 1876, when the journal was established, it had defended the American architects against the reproofs of visitors. For example, it criticized Piton in 1877 for generalizing about American work from the buildings he had seen in the Philadelphia area a year earlier.[28] By 1886, however, Europeans had reached conclusions dissimilar to those of the seventies, and the staff gloated over some of the reassessments in a very human, if unprofessional manner. "It is soothing, after the mistakes that have been made in the past by some of our foreign contemporaries in attributing to other sources the work of American architects, to find the *Builder*, in a recent issue, paying an indirect compliment to American architecture of the present day."[29] After the address of John Gass to the R.I.B.A., the journal noted that there was more discussion than usually followed a talk by a returning traveler. The discussion seemed to "indicate that American architects are in a fair way to achieve a reputation as scientific constructors—if not artists. . . ."[30] In May it reprinted a befuddled piece by Jean Boussard from *Le Moniteur des Architectes* about Richardon's Malden Library, and commented, "As we have lately read of the growing esteem in which American architecture is held in England, it will be interesting to learn how French architects regard our work."[31] Two months later the editors took an immodest bow for the entire profession when they acknowledged César Daly's compliments from "Maisons américaines":

> "One's own children are always the prettiest," and if a man's name happens casually to appear in print he is pretty sure to think that this phenomenon makes as much impression on the rest of the world as it makes on himself; but if the man himself, his words or his actions are the subject of serious discussion in the public prints there is a real reason for his feeling that the eyes of the world are turned upon him. If this is a reasonable deduction in the case of an individual it seems as though it would be equally just in the case of a class or profession.[32]

How unsophisticated this sounds today! Yet, it should be read in context. Frustrated for a decade because the venerable societies of Western architecture did not appreciate the virtues of the buildings it illustrated, the journal was unable to hide its own satisfaction, and that of the profession too, when increasingly architects abroad remarked that the work of the Americans was pertinent to their own.

Conscious of these re-evaluations and pleased with the growing maturity of their colleagues, the editors of the *American Architect* invited Paul Sédille (1836–1900), the well-known designer of the Printemps department store in Paris (1881–1889) and an authority on domestic buildings, to write an article for the journal giving his impressions of recent work in the United States. Although he procrastinated for several months—in part because he was embarrassed about his dependence on the journal itself for his information about American architecture—he finally agreed, and his article appeared in September, 1886. His evaluation, one of the more important of the decade, was later reprinted in the *Encyclopédie d'Architecture* and cited on several occasions by German critics.[33] Sédille's criticism is also important for the thesis that *L'Architecture Américaine* was one of the earliest signs of the growing French interest.

To the disappointment of the editors, Sédille wrote, "Your modern structures do not, I confess, give me complete satisfaction." His hesitation reminds us that preconceptions of long standing are not quickly dislodged and that criticism is not monolithic. He was bothered by several assumptions which American architects appeared to make: that they could mix earlier styles indiscriminately; that they did not have to respect the integrity of a classical order; that they could, without restriction, pick and choose from history's architectural treasury to suit their purposes. Though a progressive himself, Sédille still believed that "there are aesthetic laws which are and will be of all times and all countries, and to neglect them is to deprive one's self of the most essential elements of beauty." He was simply reiterating the major objection Europeans had leveled against the Americans a decade earlier: that they did not fully understand and respect the noble art of building. This criticism persisted in France and elsewhere throughout the remainder of the century. The intensity and frequency of this charge decreased slowly, but many Europeans thought that American architects would not fulfill their potential until they understood the essence of their Western architectural heritage. This was stated effectively by the *British Architect* in 1889: "When more rhythm, and fitness, proportion, and dignity are added to its originality and picturesque qualities, we shall find in American architecture something which will beat the records and earn a reputation for the nineteenth-century architect."[34] Basically, this was Sédille's conclusion. American architecture was original but not proper.

He thought the worst manifestations of these faults could be seen in the public buildings. The architects'

attempts to handle monumentality made him shiver. On this point, the planners of *L'Architecture Américaine* and Sédille agreed. They also concurred that their most satisfactory buildings were the one-family houses of the suburbs and the countryside. These houses expressed "an art truly individual which does not find its equivalent with us," he wrote. Picturesque, comfortable, and concealed by their surroundings, they appeared to be poetic solutions to domestic architecture. The shape, size and placement of the rooms, determined by the habits of the family and not by the empty rules of symmetry, resulted in an irregular plan, while the exterior, naively conceived, showed off the ingenuity of its designer. But the architects, claimed Sédille, too often made the mistake of exaggerating these effects. They sought varied, quaint facades rather than elevations conditioned by the practical necessities of the plan. Sometimes the houses looked like peasant dwellings whose ground floors were darkened by encircling verandas and whose second stories were entangled in enormous roofs. The architects' mania for animation, unsupported by good principle, was also evident within. "The rooms interpenetrate one another; they jut out at every opportunity, making angles more bizarre than agreeable." His verdict: the houses were contrived rather than logical; picturesque rather than beautiful. If the architects' penchant for overstatement was not curbed, the public would soon object and demand a return to the solid, rational forms of an earlier period. By relying upon themselves, these architects had cut themselves off from a system which would have enabled them to control the parts of the plan and the elevation, to combine one with the other and each to the whole in a pleasing and orderly manner.

## THE ONE-FAMILY, FREE-STANDING HOUSE

French opinion about the United States changed after the mid eighties. To Sédille, the designers laid all art aside when they struggled to create exotic elevations and intricate ground plans. "It is no longer architecture," he charged. But in 1892 Marcel Daly declared, "There are few nations which in architecture have achieved anything comparable to that of the United States during the past twelve years."[35] Those who objected to Sédille's criticism and presented a more positive interpretation were quite influential in the architectural milieu of Paris. In addition to Marcel Daly, then assistant editor of *La Semaine*, this group included Paul Planat, Paul Gout (1852–?), editor of the journal *L'Encyclopédie d'Architecture*, and Jean Boussard. Not all of them would have agreed with the conclusions of Daly, but, until the early nineties, they were unanimous in stating that the lessons of American architecture were best summarized in the detached, one-family houses—an aspect of American architecture clearly underscored by the photographs of *L'Architecture Américaine.*

The free-standing house intrigued these critics because it appeared to be inviting, and a pleasant place in which to raise a family, but its elevation was so fanciful, according to their standards, that they questioned whether the architect could have been entirely serious when he designed it. The first writer to admit that he was beguiled yet mystified by one of these dwellings was Jean Boussard. Late in 1885 he illustrated the house by Cass Gilbert near St. Paul, Minnesota in his *Le Moniteur* and noted that the design lacked the classicism of the preceding plate, the new buildings for the École Centrale:

> Observe the plan, the facade of this dwelling; could anything be imagined more ignorant or worse studied! Yet notice, in the midst of all this carelessness, the detail of the entrance porch, how pretty, interesting and useful. Look also at the little balcony overlooking the water, and see how pleasant life must be in that house; yet with all this—what gables on top of gables; what strange openings and curious balustrades! How an architect must have to torture his mind to invent such things.[36]

Boussard could have made the same comments about numerous plates in *L'Architecture Américaine* (III.1, 9, 30 in particular). Sédille recognized the same qualities and admitted that, momentarily, he was seduced by these unconventional forms and was delighted to see materials accentuated as decorative elements because he was tired of false ornamentation. But he finally concluded that these features were dangerous for the Americans at their stage of development because they seemed contrived. Boussard, on the other hand, was perplexed. Was it good? Was it bad? Having called the design careless and admitted that it would be hard to find one more aesthetically illiterate, he nevertheless granted that it looked pleasant and useful.

Boussard published approximately twenty-five plates of new buildings in the United States before 1893, the majority of them free-standing houses. He usually apologized for the artistic weaknesses of the examples—strange forms, odd combinations, poor proportions, unconventional ornamentation—but urged his readers not to dwell on these peculiarities. On this score, he did not agree with Sédille, who recommended, in effect, that once the architects became better educated and more sedate, they would restrain their picturesque tendencies. Boussard contended that these imaginative and overstated elevations were signs of health and not of illness. Baffled at first by American work and vacillating between condemnation and praise, he finally decided in the middle of 1886 that the French would be wiser to ponder its implications. If they could momentarily disregard the bizarre aspects, he wrote, they would find useful plans and elevations. More importantly, they would discover the values these designers honored. Citing the illustrations, Boussard argued that what mattered to the American architect was his independence and not the history of architecture. Consequently, he was freer to address problems in a contemporary, inventive

manner. His results might be less proper and learned than a French architect's, but not less workable, pleasant, or spirited. Of the three, Boussard prized spirit.

This spirit or joy or liveliness, as he also called it, impressed other French critics of the eighties. Decrying the aridity of current work at home, they pointed to the animated elevations in American architecture, even though these facades contained aesthetic infractions which Sédille and the majority of the French profession were unwilling to pardon. The argument that vitality was more important than scholarship was stated most effectively by Paul Gout at the end of the decade:

> I believe that the works of man are at times like man himself. I find that primitive works of art, incomplete, coarse, which expose the indecisiveness of inexperience or the stabbings for a procedure are often more useful, more worthy of attention, and more instructive than other works seemingly more elegant, correct in their general conception, more studied or cleverly executed, but which commit the grave error of revealing nothing to the spirit, or inspiring nothing moving or unexpected. I even claim that works of art in this category can only be admired by people of the trade who cannot afford not to take sides, whether as a consequence of their artistic education, self-interest, or bias toward a school.[37]

Gout's remarks were part of an article entitled "Maison à Boston" (see extracts below), illustrated by a plate of the Nathaniel Thayer house by Sturgis and Brigham. He explained that he liked the house, somewhat ostentatious and precious in its details, because it did not leave him indifferent. The phrase is important for an understanding of French criticism in this period. The houses the French editor chose to illustrate were usually ones to which their readers would react. *L'Architecture Américaine*'s plates summarized the biases of these critics exceptionally well. Volume three, especially, stressed houses with high and complicated elevations rather than horizontally oriented, texturally rich but plastically moderate designs preferred by later historians.

More systematic and inquisitive than the French, the Germans questioned the role of inventions in American architecture. Their journals explained the impact of the elevator on tall office buildings and publicized the devices which had been incorporated into the home to make it, in Karl Hinckeldeyn's opinion, the most successfully heated, ventilated, and sanitized dwelling in the world.[38] German critics realized that technology had increased flexibility, that central heating had made the open plan possible. They explained that the objective of the architect in the interior was a comfortable, convenient environment which met the requirements of the owner. The Germans, not the French, comprehended Sédille's insight about "rooms disposed to suit the habits of the family." In their view, the exteriors of these houses were by-products of their interiors; in fact, the house in the United States was built from the inside outward. Exaggerating the neatness of this cause-effect sequence, one observer told the Architectural and Engineering

Society of Hamburg in 1894 that one could even guess the patterns of the family by analyzing the elevation.[39] German writers appreciated the appearance of these houses and pointed out that applied ornament was obviated because the facade yielded to internal, irregular volumes. Unlike the French, however, they interpreted the exterior as an artistic outcome of internal functions.

By contrast, French critics acted as if the elevation had been an aesthetic event unaffected by the interior and unrelated to prosaic functions. The fact that none of these major critics visited the United States during this period may explain why they restricted their criticisms to the facades of the houses; illustrations, their main source of information, generally featured exteriors. But this explanation is unsatisfactory. If they had wanted to know about the interrelationships of technology, plan, and elevation, they could have found adequate material in American publications, as Marcel Daly did when he analyzed plans for the first time in a French journal in 1892.[40] They did not probe beyond the facade because they did not want to. *L'Architecture Américaine* demonstrated this very well. There were only eleven photographs of interiors, stressing wall decoration, not the flow of space or family use, and there were no plans in the three volumes. These photographs, focusing on exteriors, catered to French predilections in 1886.

## THE NATURE OF AMERICAN INFLUENCE ABROAD

Beginning in the eighties, Europeans examined the latest architecture in the United States in search of ideas beneficial to the profession in their own countries. Bascially, they were concerned with the instructive potential of a building and not with its data: its name, when it was built, where it was erected, and who designed it. While *L'Architecture Américaine* was a refreshing exception to such undocumented criticism—the table of contents listed the type, location, and architect of a building—the lists in each volume included numerous errors. German and French writers commented encouragingly about the instructive value of the architecture; the British, with whom relations had been testier, alternated between approbation and sarcasm. The *American Architect* noted this in 1889:

> We are gradually becoming wonted to having foreigners, especially Frenchmen, write amiable and appreciative criticism on the work that our architects are doing. Other foreign critics, and particularly English writers, have a way of discussing the matter *de haut en bas*, so as to leave rather more sting than balm behind; but in another column will be found a review of our present work from a German standpoint, the general trend of which is more in line with French than English comment on American architecture.[41]

To the Germans, American architecture was useful because of the high priority placed on comfort and *Zweckmässigkeit* (functionalism) and because the interior purposefulness affected exterior design. They valued this work for the cooperation between engineer and architect, for the efforts to make a building serve its users in a pleasant and convenient manner, and for its art which seemed to be imaginatively developed from function and not learnedly applied from the past. Essentially, the Germans liked the architecture because it was practical; the French because it was alive. From illustrations and photographs of one-family houses, the French concluded that the designers, however awkward, inexperienced, or immoderate, were nevertheless independent, dynamic, and bold. They cited the houses primarily to point to the vitality of the profession which produced them. From their criticisms, architecture emerges as spiritual art. Their writing suggests that they had not merely "looked" but had been affected by what they saw and that this experience could be expressed best through subjective terms like "aspiration" and "ideal." In American architecture they found signs of the revitalization of architecture and urged their colleagues to consider them seriously. To these French critics, revitalization meant a rejection of archaeological conservatism rather than the affirmation of an architecture inspired by new technology and oriented to contemporary human use. This explains their preoccupation with facades and their disinterest in the utilitarian aspects of interiors.

This criticism by the French and the Germans was pragmatic. Ultimately, it was intended to alert the respective professions to selected developments elsewhere and to prompt them to consider the advantages or disadvantages of these foreign practices for their own work. Frequently, French praise for architecture in the United States was coupled with denunciations of the current state of the art in France. Jean Boussard was the first editor to publish illustrations of American buildings with the express purpose of pointing out weaknesses at home. On at least four occasions in 1886, when he included plates of American buildings in *Le Moniteur*, he declared his opposition to the dryness and formal banality of contemporary French buildings and promised to combat "this funeral error" by publishing illustrations from the United States.[42] Between 1886 and 1888 he often encouraged his audience to imitate the attitudes which shaped American architecture or stated that he would be pleased to see the day when such uninhibited designs appeared in France. He repeatedly selected illustrations of upper middle-class, detached houses as the most attractive examples of this "curiously instructive" work. At the end of the decade, noting a stylistic revolution in the United States, he began to illustrate larger, classically influenced houses, several of which contradicted his generalizations of a few years earlier.

Because Paul Gout's article about the Nathaniel Thayer house demonstrates so well the way in which some critics used American work as a whip to flog their friends, it should be read closely. He created for his readers a hypothetical situation in which a judge would be asked to choose between two buildings. It was obvious that the judge was really the profession in France and the two buildings examples of French and American work respectively:

> I submit that the first of the two buildings upon which our imaginary judge will declare himself is a pure masterpiece as the classical school understands it, that is, from the point of view of the combination and adjustment of formulas purified by the infallible taste of several generations of academicians. Correctness of proportions, purity of line, firmness of profiles, fullness of forms, everything is present in the proper measure to satisfy the demands of the most refined taste. It is like a magnificent garment of another age on a man of today, like the coat of a Byzantine emperor, laden with gold and rich with jewels, on the bony back of some dissolute of the roulette wheel or the boulevard.
>
> Then the second one which testifies to the most complete ignorance of the conventional forms with which edifices are usually composed according to the dictates of classical authorities. The general outlines are based on concerns for the material order which do not look beyond a program practical for architecture. The form is simply what its function in the structure permits it to be. The profiles are designed according to their use and do not reveal a precious respect for modelling. In brief, it is a work which denotes in its creator a rusticity, certainly regrettable, but mitigated by an evident intention to do well, by the search based on needs, and by a basic sincerity and goodwill offered in compensation for a lack of urbanity and a lack of etiquette that outrages the classical eye.
>
> In the first instance then, are beautiful forms envisaged in themselves, or, at the very least, forms which one acknowledges to be beautiful by virtue of their being molded and remolded in order to fit the formula of official art, but which in reality express nothing, respond to no practical idea, and yield to no rational exigency. In the second, are the blemished forms of unskillfulness and inexperience, but nevertheless, sincere, reasonable, and utilitarian. In the first instance, fine manners, a language that is acknowledged to be proper although it expresses nothing in its politeness of conventions trained by aristocratic habits; in the second, primitive conduct, a clumsy attitude, expressions bizarre in their rusticity, but at heart, sane ideas, a sincere sentiment, and in spirit independent and steady.[43]

Gout explained that if he had been the judge, he would not have had the slightest hesitation. He then referred his readers to the Thayer house, calling it an incomplete but adequate illustration of his position:

> It may contain enough to jolt an architect deeply enamoured of classical methods of composition. As for me, despite certain weaknesses in the details, I find in it a sincerity, a look of independence, something personal and picturesque that does not leave me indifferent. Simply by examining these facades, I sense a concern with making the elevations and the openings conform to the interior plan and arrangement of the building.

> Doubtlessly, the orthodoxy of the classical orders is disregarded here: I looked in vain for the fluid lines, strong entablatures and sonorous motifs for which official teaching had prepared me. But to the contrary, I find here an artistic treatment, which, without being new, adapts itself flexibly to the naive, sincere and expressive designs of a frank and rational structure.
>
> Why must such lessons of good sense come to us from America?[44]

Several journalists, then, notably Boussard, Gout, and Marcel Daly, brandished American examples as weapons to drive French architects from positions they considered reactionary. They did not approach American architecture as disinterested critics but as frustrated nationalists concerned about the inability of their profession to develop an architecture appropriate for late nineteenth-century French life. Because they were frustrated, their remarks were frequently categorical and expansive. They overstated faults at home and virtues abroad. French work was moribund; American throbbing and promising. In France the purpose of a building was subordinate to arid aesthetics; in the United States design and utility were interrelated. French architects looked backward; the Americans forward. Moreover, the French image of the role of the architect in the United States was not realistic. Most English commentators depicted him as one who accepted the will of the public and who was prepared to defer to the logic of the engineer if it were more efficient or economical to do so. Though sensitive and ingenious, he was, nevertheless, an individual deeply affected by his culture. By contrast, the French tended to envision him, not as a cork on the water, but a genius who determined his destiny. Independent and aloof, he was immune to the cautionary pressures of the common horde. Paul Planat's *Encyclopédie de l'Architecture* defined him as a "seeker, original and bold, whose free spirit and release from classical ideas and ignorant conventions of prejudices and systems enable him to respond to his program practically."[45] According to Marcel Daly:

> The American advances without turning his head. Not chained to the artistic ways of his ancestors, he does not search for rules in the past; he sees only an arsenal of forms from which he draws freely thus creating the most unexpected and also the most bizarre effects, for his liberty often leads to license. The spontaneous genius of the American is repulsed by copying, even by adaptation.[46]

Even Daly, who dug more deeply than other critics, minimized societal factors affecting American architecture and glorified the individual designers as if they waged lonely battles against incumbent rules. Of all of the observers abroad, the French were most likely to emphasize the role of the architect and to de-emphasize social and economic influences which shape architecture.

If these men overstated the case, they did so purposefully. They also picked carefully from the American scene, singling out aspects pertinent to their theses and glossing over or pardoning, as indiscretions of the innocent, those which were inappropriate or unimpressive. Ironically, the part of American work they valued least was the final product—the building: domestic, public, religious or commercial. Even the houses, which received the best press, were rarely called beautiful. The adjectives commonly applied to them were "bizarre," "strange," "eccentric," "curious." In recent years several historians have attempted to prove the influence of American work abroad by pointing to buildings in Europe which exhibit visual similarities to buildings erected earlier in the United States. This architecture was influential abroad in the late nineteenth century and there is stylistic evidence to support the statement; however, it was influential primarily because of its methods and attitudes. The process—not the building—was coveted.

Europeans shuddered at the thought of importing an American-designed building. In countless speeches and articles in the late eighties and nineties, a returning visitor would state that he certainly hoped he would never see the day when a "Yankee building" disturbed the beauty of his favorite city. Above all, they feared the transplanted skyscraper. Few critics in this period advocated the tall building for their own cities. One exception was Adolphe Bocage (1860–?), a French delegate to the Chicago Exposition, who guardedly wrote, "At the risk of being reproached for Utopian thinking, I dare to foresee the possibility of a skyscraper system, even for middle-class domestic architecture, of a 'reasonable' height and spaced at a distance from each other like modern monuments along our major streets." [47] He rightly predicted the idea would be condemned to the realm of fantasy. Though much less disturbing, the house—especially the frame dwelling—was also unwanted. The French preferred the appearance of the houses in wood to those in stone because they thought wood exerted less restraint on the picturesque inclination of Americans. But wood was not a material of which legendary architecture was built. And what protection did a shell of clapboards or shingles afford? Compared to the substantial houses of France in which generations of families had lived, the frame house looked cheap and temporary. For these reasons, *La Semaine des Constructeurs* was dumbfounded to discover that Grover Cleveland, the first citizen of the United States, spent his time away from Washington in a house of wood. [48] The only Frenchman to write that the frame building might be imported was Marcel Daly, but his numerous qualifications expose the unconventionality of his suggestion: "Perhaps it could be adopted advantageously in certain of our provinces, for example, in temporary structures housing railroad workers...." [49] Even those partial to the United States, in France and elsewhere, wanted to protect their soil from desecration by buildings which looked like they had been designed across the water.

America's contribution to international architecture in this period should not be measured primarily by the number of buildings erected in Europe which were reminiscent of designs planned or executed earlier in the United States. Paul Gout pinpointed the real contribution

when he wrote in 1891, "In America the liberty of institutions seems to have meant the liberty of art. When will France enjoy the same privilege?" [50] For Gout, the value of American architecture was not to be found in its final products but in the architects' freedom to solve problems on their terms. He envied them because they appeared to be free to scorn history, proven methods, artistic etiquette and academies, free to believe in themselves despite their inadequate schooling and experience, free to take risks and make mistakes and free to rearrange traditional priorities to meet new challenges. These freedoms hardly guaranteed great buildings. At their most generous, the French had dubbed them "picturesque." What fascinated Gout, Boussard and Marcel Daly, however, was the absence of the conventions, obligations and preconceptions which would have protected the intelligent French designer from creating the "bizarre" and "curious" buildings found in American periodicals. Seemingly uninhibited and unencumbered, the Americans could attack their problems directly. Because they owed so little to the past, they could be receptive to new approaches, techniques, inventions and materials. We have seen that the image of the American architect in France was inflated. The French exalted his independence to dramatize their charges that the profession at home had not declared its independence from traditions which, in their opinions, were now inimical to the art. They called American practice healthy and the French sick, a comparison restated just as simplistically and dogmatically for German architects by the critic Hans Schliepmann (1856–1929): "There lies the future, here the floundering past. There lies freshness, here the Academy." [51] The Americans had not developed the long-awaited modern architecture; they had progressed to principles which, some claimed, promised the best chances of eventual success, and these principles were well publicized around 1890 in France and elsewhere in Europe despite widespread reservations about the buildings they produced.

## RICHARDSON AND EUROPEAN CRITICS

Although the French praised the American profession, they rarely mentioned individual architects. For them, American designers were nameless, free spirits. Even Paul Sédille, the author of the longest evaluation of the mid eighties, acted as if the buildings were created anonymously. He cited only one architect, Richard Morris Hunt, because he accommodated "elegant and distinguished architecture" to the "exigencies of life," and only two buildings—his Henry G. Marquand and William K. Vanderbilt houses in New York—because they were designed in a style "at once free and measured." [52] The French overlooked specific architects and specific buildings for two main reasons. They had not traveled to the United States to meet individual architects and visit their buildings; instead, they relied on illustrations, a less personalized source. Secondly, the differences between one architect and another in the United States seemed insignificant and unimportant compared to those which clearly differentiated French and American practice. For their purpose, the French could generalize from one illustrated example as easily as from another. Neither the name of the architect nor the peculiarities of his style were as important to them as the plate's effectiveness in summarizing the American touch.

British critics of the eighties also focused on the essence rather than the personalities of American architecture. They occasionally mentioned Hunt by name and around 1890 often referred to the most astounding buildings of Chicago, the Masonic Temple and the Auditorium, but usually ommitted reference to their designers—Burnham and Root and Adler and Sullivan. They de-emphasized the significance of an individual or a firm for another reason: there were simply too many of them. The *British Architect* in 1889 apologized frankly, "We cannot remember all those who are responsible for the best and most original work in America."[53] To cover this unprofessional admission, the editors then referred vaguely to the work of Leroy Buffington, W. R. Emerson, Peabody and Stearns, McKim, Mead and White, Rotch and Tilden, and "others." The journal *Building* coped with the difficult challenge of finding the leadership of the American profession by praising twenty-three individuals and firms for their recent work.[54] In 1890, the British could not discuss intelligently the leading architects of the country; they could only state that there appeared to be many of them and their work was impressive.

Henry Hobson Richardson was the sole exception to the generalization that the American architect was treated as an anonymous artist. The British discovered Richardson late in his career. He was probably unknown to the editors of the *British Architect* in 1883 when they misattributed three of his buildings to Peabody and Stearns, of Boston.[55] The establishment of British architecture first acknowledged his talent during the 1886 exhibition arranged by John B. Gass at the R.I.B.A.[56] Shortly thereafter, he was invited to serve as an honorary and corresponding member of the Society. Two other events of this time fixed his reputation in Britain: the *American Architect's* poll of the best buildings of the United States and, ironically, his death in April of 1886. The British did not pick up the significance of the 1885 poll immediately, but, as soon as Richardson died, they cited the results— he had designed five of the first ten, including the "best," Trinity Church in Boston—to prove that he had been at the head of the profession. Secondly, his death affected the attitude of several British critics who had overlooked him during his lifetime.[57] To make amends for this omission, they overcompensated by discussing Richardson as if he were the only American architect. Suddenly, American architecture—at least for some critics—was no longer devoid of personalities; Richardson and his buildings became the proof of broad statements.

English architects and critics did not agree about the precise role which Richardson had played. A few argued that he was the most competent and inventive of a new American school in which the level of talent was surprisingly high. The majority, however, preferred to regard him as an exception, the lone master among many eager beginners. According to this viewpoint, Richardson was mainly responsible for the changes and improvements noticeable in American work. In 1888 Alfred Waterhouse (1830–1905), President of the R.I.B.A., observed, "He seems to have created a new-born interest in architecture in America . . . [and] he has left behind him a school of young Americans who appear to be following in his steps in developing the capabilities of Romanesque Art. . . ."[58] English writers mentioned Richardson frequently after 1885. Initially, they did not discuss him in the context of architectural history. He was an able designer, certainly, but they were reluctant to assign to him a place in Western architecture or to predict his future influence. In the middle of the decade, they commended him for his "breadth and boldness of treatment," or for his "strongly-marked individuality." By 1888 a few were calling him one of the most important architects of the nineteenth century. Now he was sometimes referred to as a "genius," a "master," and an "artist."

Richardson's reputation abroad was based almost entirely upon the external appearance of his buildings. Between 1886 and 1888, the British said little about his skill in planning, the finish of his interiors, or his ability to accommodate the structure to the purpose. When Waterhouse summarized the high points of Richardon's work, he emphasized its visual qualities:

> These peculiarities appear to be chiefly the discarding of the orders, the Romanesque feeling, admirable planning, appearance of strength and solidity, the value put upon mere wall surface whenever attainable, the treatment of this surface by the varied coursing of stonework, and the contrast between tooled and rough surfaces; the use of coloured materials, especially of stone of different hues; battered bases, sparing use of strong courses, the introduction of deep voussoirs, the rounding of salient angles and a leaning to circular forms on plan.[59]

English writers did not explain the meaning of "originality" when they applied the word to Richardson's architecture. Did "originality" connote a radical departure from past architecture or did it mean that he found in history a vocabulary for contemporary architectural expression? Opinions were mixed and usually unclear. "Genius recognizes no fixed rules. Richardson threw aside all tradition, and, having solved his problems both in design and construction in his own way, succeeded in striking a key-note in architectural composition that will continue to vibrate through the length and breadth of the United States," declared the *Journal of Proceedings of the R.I.B.A.* in 1888.[60] Richardson's friend and classmate at the École des Beaux-Arts in 1859, R. Phené Spiers (1838–1916), also stressed the revolutionary character of his work. Referring to the photographs and drawings exhibited by John Gass in 1886, he concluded that "It would have been impossible for an English architect to have dared to go to that extent; he would have had against him the criticism of all those who are afraid of sinning against the laws of recognized archaeology."[61] On the other hand, some critics claimed his architecture was traditional; his designs represented a skillful, powerful adaptation of Romanesque motifs to the architectural demands of the nineteenth century. His originality was the originality of adaptation, a conclusion which did not diminish his achievement, as several pointed out, because an entirely new style of architecture was an unlikely, if not impossible dream.

Between 1886 and 1888 British journals mentioned Richardson as frequently as any Continental architect, and in May of 1886 the *Builder* even asserted that he had gained a widespread reputation on the Continent.[62] But the recognition of the establishment was withheld; the R.I.B.A. cautiously awarded its Medal to designers whose scholarship, rather than imagination, provoked admiration. Before announcing the winner of the 1888 Gold Medal, Theophilus von Hansen of Vienna, Waterhouse explained that Richardson, unfortunately, had died before his architecture was thoroughly known in Britain, and, consequently, his name had not been listed among those eligible for the award.[63] Despite his high standing with some professionals in Britain, others, aware that his fame had spread quickly after his death, were not sure whether he was an overnight sensation or a solid, confidence-inspiring architect. Their suspicions were nourished by the realization that he was a product of the artistically weak American profession. If the aesthetic limitations of his environment enhanced his uniqueness, they also made judgments abroad more difficult.

At the turn of the decade, the English still considered Richardson America's finest architect but opinions about his architecture underwent a slow transformation. In 1886 he had been characterized as an American mutation; in 1890 he was treated as an architect within the Western tradition. The magical aura which surrounded him earlier faded, but his stature continued to grow. The question of whether or not he had authored a new style was never settled. Most critics preferred a middle course, granting that both originality and tradition had been the foundation of his architecture. Robert Kerr wrote a representative British opinion in 1891: if it were possible to have architectural originality in the present day, Richardson would be the most likely candidate for the honor, "but it is quite enough if we are able to say that he derived his inspiration from an unusual source, and employed his imitative genius in an unusual manner."[64]

Some negative criticism also appeared. Because the quality of American design had not declined noticeably after Richardson, some critics abroad modified original judgments about his relative importance to the profession. A few even claimed his influence had not been beneficial. Occasionally, he was attacked for making his houses look too primitive or charged with seeking new forms at the expense of sound composition. The *British Architect* in January 1889 rebuked him for his artistic idiosyncrasies: "So we find in his designs things which never ought to occur beyond the stage of pupilage, such as similar features of different sizes and proportions in the same facade, a plethora of enrichment in one part unbalanced by corresponding value elsewhere, juxtaposition of features which do not harmonize,—and so on."[65] Some thought his architecture was too private to be redeveloped by lesser talents and predicted that his success would ultimately be a negative influence on his surviving contemporaries. They argued that his followers committed the fatal error of mastering his forms without possessing his unifying sensibilities. Horace Townsend, who had spent twelve years in the United States and was the most active publicist for Richardson when he returned to Britain in 1890, told the Architectural Association in 1891 that the United States was swarming with "little tin Richardsons on wheels . . . marked by all the vices but giving only pale reflection of the virtues of the original."[66] However, the majority of British and Continental critics agreed that, despite weaker restatements, at least his students and imitators were inspired by fine models.

The only obituary of Richardson published on the Continent in 1886 was written by Karl Hinckeldeyn, who was still associated with the German Embassy in the United States.[67] He called Richardson's death a tragic loss, for he was not only the country's finest contemporary architect but also the most creative in its history. While British critics tended to see American architecture in Richardson's image, Hinckeldeyn carefully distinguished between his architecture and that of others. Richardson was exceptional; the others mediocre. Generally displeased with American work in 1886, he predicted that its post-Richardson period would be a gloomy one. However, in 1892 he declared that the long-standing German view that the arts did not flourish in the United States was true no longer, at least in the field of architecture.[68] Richardson, he explained, was primarily responsible for this transformation. Other German critics in the eighties did not emphasize the importance of Richardson as strongly as did Hinckeldeyn. Eventually, they were to agree that he had been the foremost American designer of the late nineteenth century, but they reached this conclusion when many of them came to the United States for the World's Columbian Exposition in 1893.

The French did not know about Richardson's reputation in the United States, nor had they learned about the results of the *American Architect*'s poll. Furthermore, no professional journal reported his death. Jean Boussard referred to him simply as an American architect in his confused remarks about the Malden Library in 1886.[69] But for *L'Architecture Américaine*, we could conclude that the French failed to recognize his distinctive touch just as they had failed to single out other architects in the United States. However, André, Daly fils et C$^{ie}$ chose eight Richardson buildings— the most informative pictorial survey of his achievements published abroad during the decade. At a time when most Europeans emphasized the collective traits in American architecture, *L'Architecture Américaine* offered an informative register of the country's leading designers.

## ARCHITECTURAL PHOTOGRAPHY

*L'Architecture Américaine* is a fine example of architectural photography in the late nineteenth century. Peter Collins has written, in his challenging *Changing Ideas of Modern Architecture*, that European journals first used photographs in 1856. Thereafter they were less dependent on the architect's drawings and tended to select architecture which could be flattered by the camera. However, costs and habit restricted the number of photographic reproductions for several decades. Though not established until 1876, the *American Architect* was one of the first professional journals to use photographs extensively. To increase circulation, in 1884 it began to issue, on a regular basis, full-page gelatine prints of European monuments as well as the most imposing examples of American work. These photographs contributed to the standardization of taste at home and won acclaim abroad. The *British Architect* advised its readers "to procure all the numbers of this journal which contain gelatine prints of European architecture. They have formed an interesting feature of the *American Architect* during the past year and when collected would form a valuable little folio in themselves." [70] Encouraged, in March 1886 the *American Architect* announced an international issue, titled the "Imperial Edition," each volume of which included forty gelatine prints and thirty-six double-page photolithographic prints. In 1886 there were few European architectural journals which could match the *American Architect*'s success in architectural photography.

In Europe, British journals issued more photographs than German journals and many more than the French during the eighties and early nineties. Generally, photographs were reserved for buildings which were historically important, excellently designed, or highly unusual. At first European editors did not select American buildings for photographic plates. As a consequence of increased attention, they published them occasionally. If a photograph implied architectural quality, then the British thought Henry Richardson was the most important designer in the country, for two of his buildings, Austin Hall at Harvard and the Winn Memorial Library at Woburn, were among the earliest photographs of American work. [71] After 1886, photographs of buildings in the United States were issued more frequently, many of them taken from the *American Architect* and the *Inland Architect* of Chicago. Through its photographs, engravings, sketches, notes, articles, and reprints, the architectural journal in Britain, Germany, France, and the United States was the chief medium in the eighties encouraging the concept of a Western international architecture, bridging both sides of the Atlantic.

*L'Architecture Américaine* is a document of this wider-based, international movement. It also provides us with a sample of architectural photography in the 1880s. The publishers would not have used photography to survey a body of architecture which had been dismissed, mocked, or severely criticized unless photographing buildings had become a relatively common art. If processing costs had been very high, they probably would have decided against issuing one hundred and twenty plates, knowing that the audience for the project would be limited. The photographs vary in quality, but they are generally clear and quite informative. Although weak in coping with movement and variations of light, they register details and textures surprisingly well. *L'Architecture Américaine* was an early photograph study of the monuments of a region, but far from the earliest; the first of this genre was probably Maxime du Camp's, *Egypte, Nubie, Palestine et Syrie; Dessins Photographiques*, Paris, 1852. Among similar studies of American monuments, *L'Architecture Américaine* was one of the earliest, and among those, probably the most diversified. In the middle of the decade American presses published similar collections, the best known of which were Appleton's *Artistic Houses*, 2 volumes, New York, 1883–84, Sheldon's *Artistic Country Seats*, 2 volumes, New York, 1886–87, and the *Monographs of American Architecture* Series which commenced in 1885.

## FRENCH CRITICISM AFTER 1893

The image of architecture in the United States presented to the French by *L'Architecture Américaine* was not seriously challenged until 1893. Until this date the articles published in *La Semaine*, *La Construction Moderne*, and other Parisian journals restated earlier conclusions: that American architecture, if ingenuous and unorthodox, was nevertheless spirited and that the domestic work revealed these traits better than any other type of building. In 1893 numerous French architects and critics attended Chicago's World's Columbian Exposition. They now had the opportunity to examine buildings directly instead of judging them through illustrations in American or French journals. As a result, the French became better acquainted with the leading names of the American profession. They paid tribute to Hunt for serving as a missionary of French architectural theory to the New World and praised the surface treatment of the buildings of Louis Sullivan. Although Richardson had died seven years earlier, they also discovered his work.

Writers were better informed about the appearance and the function of the interiors of the buildings once they had entered them. Consequently, the criticism of 1893 and later years was generally more diversified and statistically richer. Increasingly, the French tried to explain the relationships between the way Americans chose to live and work and the architecture created to meet these particular demands. If the architect of the eighties had been viewed as a free spirit who painted uninhibited, refreshing elevations, he was now depicted as an artist who tried to make his buildings convenient and comfortable. Jacques Hermant (1855–1930), a French delegate to the Exposition and the most perspective critic of the first half of the nineties, argued that the American was not a creator of picturesque facades; to the contrary, he was a most practical individual who had exploited science liberally and had shaped the art of the future: "scientific art." [72]

Because the Yankee buildings of the eighties did not conform to aesthetic conventions which some French critics considered worn-out and restrictive, these critics had glamorized the American architect as one without prejudices who was free to express himself despite the possibility of embarrassing results. He pushed aside classical rules, they claimed. But when the French arrived in 1893, they discovered that he had not divested himself of that urge to stand with the Romans and the Greeks. They were not pleased with the classical revival. They acknowledged it during the remainder of the nineties,

and occasionally reminded their readers that the American students at the École des Beaux Arts had been loyal to their teachers and were currently artistic ambassadors for France, but they did not often discuss buildings of the revival. Attracted in the eighties by unclassical, picturesque houses, they concentrated in the nineties on tall office buildings, particularly those in Chicago which were less noticeably affected by the new movement than those in New York. They wrote admiringly about the collaboration between architects and engineers in the United States and supplied examples to prove that technology could make architectural wonders possible. Yet the image of the American architect as a "seeker, original, and bold" or one who "advances without turning his head" was shattered by the classical revival. For a brief moment, between the middle of the eighties and 1893, the editors of the leading architectural journals of France thought the American architect understood principles and exhibited attitudes which would lead to the long-sought modern architecture, but they overestimated his independence and unconsciously substituted their goals for his. During the nineties the American architect continued to provide "lessons of good sense," but he was no longer on the pedestal to which French critics had momentarily elevated him.

# NOTES

1. César Daly, "Maisons américaines," *Revue Générale de l'Architecture et des Travaux Publics*, ser. 4, XIII (1886), 23.

2. César Daly, "L'Amérique à la recherche d'un procédé de délassement," *Revue Générale de l'Architecture et des Travaux Publics*, ser. 4, X (1883), 83.

3. César Daly, "Maisons américaines," 23.

4. C. Piton, "Lettres de Philadelphie," *Revue Générale de l'Architecture et des Travaux Publics*, ser. 4, IV (1877), 167–173, 231–238, and 254–259.

5. Rudler & Delmas, "Exposition universelle de 1878," *Encyclopédie d'Architecture*, ser. 2, VII (1878), 38.

6. P. Planat, "Chronique: La caisse des écoles," *La Semaine des Constructeurs*, I (March 17, 1877), 422.

7. "Cottage à Dell Wood (Angleterre)," *Le Moniteur des Architectes*, new ser., XIX (1885), 144. This house, designed for Kirby Barnum near St. Paul by Cass Gilbert, was mistakenly located in England. The illustration was first published in the *American Architect*, XVII (January 17, 1885), 31.

8. C. Piton, 167.

9. "The *American Architect*," *British Architect*, XXI (April 11, 1884), 179. The American journal had written uncomplimentarily about the ventilation system installed in the Church of St. John, Wilton Road, London.

10. "The Godwin Bursary 1882: Tour in the United States," *Royal Institute of British Architects, Proceedings*, V (December 21, 1882), 45.

11. See "Iron architecture in the United States," *Architect*, XXVIII (December 30, 1882), 407–408; "Sky building in New York," *Building News*, VL (September 7, 1883), 363–364; "Very tall building," *Architect*, XXX (September 15, 1883), 155–156; "Buildings and fittings in the United States," *Builder*, VL (September 29, 1883), 407–408; and "The architectural employment of iron," *Architect*, XXXI (March 22, 1884), 185–186.

12. John B. Gass, "Some American methods," *Royal Institute of British Architects, Transactions*, new ser., II (1885–1886), 143–144.

13. "Architecture thirty years hence," *British Architect*, XXIII (February 13, 1885), 82.

14. "The London *Builder's* appreciation of American architecture," *American Architect*, XIX (January 2, 1886), 2.

15. For references to Lange's address, see "Verschiedenes," *Allgemeine Zeitung*, No. 240 (August 29, 1884), 3541–3542; Fr. Lange, "Das Bauwesen in den Vereinigten Staaten von Nordamerika," *Centralblatt der Bauverwaltung*, IV (September 3, 1884), 355–358 and (September 6, 1884), 365–366; Lange, "Das Bauwesen in den Vereinigten Staaten von Nordamerika," *Schweizerische Bauzeitung*, IV (September 13, 1884), 70–72; (September 20, 1884), 78–79; (September 27, 1884), 84–85; (October 4, 1884), 87–89; and "Das Bauwesen in den Vereinigten Staaten von Nordamerika," *Deutsche Bauzeitung*, XVIII (November 15, 1884), 550–551; (November 22, 1884), 560–562; (November 29, 1884), 571–574; (December 3, 1884), 577–579.

16. These views appeared in the following articles in the *Centralblatt der Bauverwaltung*: "Vermischtes: Das Washington-Denkmal," IV (December 28, 1884), 558 and "Das

Washington-Denkmal in der Hauptstadt der Vereinigten Staaten," V (June 6, 1885), 236–237; "Die Welt-Ausstellung in New Orleans 1884–85," V (July 18, 1885), 308–309 and (July 25, 1885), 315–317; "Leuchtthurm bei Port Sanilac am Huron-See im Staate Michigan," V (September 5, 1885), 373; "Die Begründung eines Verbandes der 'Architekten des Westens' in Nordamerica," V (January 24, 1885), 38–40; and "Zur Handhabung der Baupolizei in New-York," V (May 23, 1885), 206–207.

17. Paul Graef and Karl Hinckeldeyn, *Neubauten in Nordamerika* (Berlin, 1897).

18. Raymond Daly, "Richard Morris Hunt," *La Semaine des Constructeurs*, ser. 3, I (August 24, 1895), 217–218.

19. Marcel Daly signed the following articles in *La Semaine des Constructeurs*: "Un coffre-fort monumental," X (January 9, 1886), 330–332; "Villas et maisons de campaigne américaines," X (June 12, 1886), 594–596; "Construction sur mauvais soil," ser. 2, II (April 28, 1888), 519–520; "Les constructions en bois aux États-Unis," ser. 2, III (September 1, 1888), 112; "L'Architecture américaine," ser. 2, VI (April 23, 1892), 515–517; (April 30, 1892), 532–533; (May 7, 1892), 544.

20. The *Deutsche Bauzeitung*, December 14, 1895, announced that at last German readers could expect a thorough study of American architecture and industrial arts because Max Junghändel was currently in New York preparing a manuscript on these subjects. Junghändel had gained a limited reputation as an architectural historian with his studies of the buildings of Spain and of Egypt. "We hope that the American architects will gladly grant to his meritorious and very promising undertaking the necessary support and assistance," added the editors. A week later the *Bauzeitung* explained that the book had been planned for some time by the firm of Julius Becker of Berlin. The proposed title was *Die Baukunst Nordamerikas* and the date of publication 1896. There is no evidence that the title was published, but the groundwork of Junghändel may have been used by Graef and Hinckeldeyn in *Neubauten in Nordamerika*, published a year later by the same firm. The *Inland Architect* of Chicago mentioned a second, apparently unpublished effort in February 1895. Reviewing an address by Victor Champier, editor of *Revue des Arts Décoratifs*, before the Conservatory of Arts and Sciences in Paris, the journal stated that Champier had recently written a history of American architecture. There is no evidence to support this assertion.

21. "American architecture winning attention in Europe," *American Architect*, XXIII (March 17, 1888), 122.

22. "Maison de campagne près de New York," *La Semaine des Constructeurs*, ser. 2, II (February 18, 1888), 401.

23. I have located two copies of *L'Architecture Américaine*. The Free University of Berlin owned one until 1967 when it was apparently lost. The Architektur Sammlung of the Technical University of Munich now holds the only known extant copy.

24. Carl Condit, *The Chicago School of Architecture* (Chicago, 1964), 59.

25. See John B. Gass, "The Godwin Bursary: Portions of a report of a visit to the United States of America and Canada," *Royal Institute of British Architects, Transactions*, new ser., II (1885–1886), 145–162 for the plans of three floors of the Home Insurance Building by W. L. B. Jenney. See also "The Home Insurance Building," *Irish Builder*, XXVIII (May 15, 1886), 143 for an illustrated elevation of this building.

26. For information about Bing see *Artistic America, Tiffany Glass and Art Nouveau* (Cambridge, 1970), which includes an introduction by Robert Koch.

27. This phrase was used frequently beginning in 1886. Jean Boussard coined the phrase: "American architecture is exceedingly interesting to study in its manifold transformations; borrowing as it does from every style, from every form, from every epoch, its monuments are curiously instructive," in "American architecture as seen by the French," *American Architect*, XIX (May 1, 1886), 209–210, a translation from "Bibliothèque publique à Malden, Mass.," *Le Moniteur des Architectes*, new ser., XX (1886), 46–47.

28. "American architecture from a French standpoint," *American Architect*, II (December 22, 1877), 408.

29. "The London *Builder's* appreciation of American architecture," 2.

30. "American architecture as seen by English architects," *American Architect*, XIX (April 10, 1886), 175.

31. "American architecture as seen by the French," 209.

32. "American architectrue as seen by foreigners," *American Architect*, XX (July 17, 1886), 26.

33. Paul Sédille, "American architecture from a French standpoint," *American Architect*, XX (September 11, 1886), 122–124. The article later was reprinted as "Lettres sur Amérique," *Encyclopédie d'Architecture*, ser. 3, V (1886–1887), 11–16. Sedille was subsequently quoted in Mühlke, "Das amerikanische Landhaus und die Preisbewerbung des '*American Architect*,'" *Centralblatt der Bauverwaltung*, VII (January 8, 1887), 11 and by Karl Hinckeldeyn in *Neubauten in Nordamerika*, 2.

34. "American architecture," *British Architect*, XXXI (January 18, 1889), 47.

35. Marcel Daly, "L'Architecture américaine," 515.

36. "American 'picturesque architecture' as seen from a French standpoint," *American Architect*, XVIII (November 14, 1885), 230.

37. Paul Gout, "Maison à Boston," *Encyclopédie d'Architecture*, ser. 4, I (1888–1889), 132.

38. K. Hinckeldeyn, "Hochbau-Constructionen und innerer Ausbau in den Vereinigten Staaten," *Centralblatt der Bauverwaltung*, VII (March 19, 1887), 117.

39. Cl., "Arch.-und Ing. Verein zu Hamburg," *Deutsche Bauzeitung*, XXVIII (January 24, 1894), 43.

40. Marcel Daly, "L'Architecture américaine," 532–533, 544.

41. "Foreigners' views of American architecture," *American Architect*, XXV (May 25, 1889), 242.

42. See the following articles in *Le Moniteur des Architectes* in 1886: "Mercantile Trust and Deposit Co., Baltimore, Maryland," new ser., XX, 48; "Architecture américaine: Types de porches," new ser., XX, 80; "Villa Mauresque en Amérique," new ser., XX, 128; and "Hôtel à Clifton," new ser., XX, 175.

43. Paul Gout, "Maison à Boston," 133.

44. *Ibid.*

45. Brincourt, "États-Unis," *Encyclopédie de l'Architecture et de la Construction*, IV, 2 (1888–1895), 423.

46. Marcel Daly, "L'Architecture américaine," 515.

47. Adolphe Bocage, "L'Architecture aux États-Unis," *L'Architecture*, VII (October 13, 1894), 338. Another

exception was the author of "Les hautes maisons américaines," *La Construction Moderne*, VII (November 14, 1891), 69, who also suggested that if these buildings were placed far apart on wide avenues they would be suitable for French cities.

48. F. Monmory, "Maison de campagne de M. Grover Cleveland," *La Semaine des Constructeurs*, ser. 2, I (January 29, 1887), 364.

49. Marcel Daly, "Les constructions en bois aux États-Unis," 112.

50. Paul Gout, "Maison américaine," *Encyclopédie d'Architecture*, ser. 4, IV (1891–1892), 21.

51. Hans Schliepmann, "Amerikanische Architektur," *Kunstwart*, VII (August, 1894), 339.

52. Paul Sédille, 123.

53. "American architecture," *British Architect*, XXXI (January 18, 1889), 47.

54. "American architecture," *Building*, VIII (April 28, 1888), 133–134. The journal cited the following architects: J. Calvin Stevens, C. Howard Walker, Wm. C. Hazlett, Rossiter and Wright, Charles A. Gifford, Berg and Clark, George Martin Huss, Sidney Smith, M. C. Beers, Schaub and Berlin, J. Cochran, Bauer and Hill, F. Schock, Cobb and Frost, George H. Edbrooke, L. B. Dixon, Weston and Tuckerman, Henry F. Kilburn, McKim, Mead and White, W. R. Emerson, C. S. Luce, Cabot and Chandler, and Treat and Folz.

55. See "Modern American architecture," *British Architect*, XIX (January 5, 1883), 7. The three buildings were the Library and Town Hall at North Easton and the Library at Quincy, Mass. The *British Architect* corrected the error in "Modern American architecture," XIX (March 30, 1883), 154–155.

56. Richardson buildings exhibited at the R.I.B.A., according to partial information supplied by Gass, were the following: Staircase at Albany; Town Hall, North Easton; Crane Library, Quincy; Memorial Library, Woburn; Brattle Square Church, Boston; Store, Boston; House, Cambridge; State House, North Easton; Sever Hall, Harvard; Monograph on Austin Hall, Harvard; Trinity Church, Boston; Allegheny Court House; Pittsburgh; City Hall, Albany; Y.M.C.A. Building, Buffalo (project); Norseman

Fountain (sketch); Episcopal Cathedral (proposed); and the Capitol, Albany. For a partial list of the 130 drawings and photographs exhibited, see *Royal Institute of British Architects, Journal of Proceedings*, new ser., II (1886), 161–162.

57. British obituaries were, "The late H. H. Richardson," *Architect*, XXXV (May 21, 1886), 306–307; "The late H. H. Richardson, of Brookline, Mass.," *Building News*, L (May 21, 1886), 817–818; and "Royal Institute of British Architects," *Builder*, L (May 22, 1886), 740.

58. "The President's address, Royal Institute of British Architects," *Builder*, LV (November 10, 1888), 338.

59. *Ibid*.

60. "The late Mr. Richardson," *Royal Institute of British Architects, Journal of Proceedings*, new ser., IV (February 8, 1888), 141.

61. John B. Gass, "Some American methods," *Royal Institute of British Architects, Journal of Proceedings*, new ser., II (March 18, 1886), 184.

62. "Royal Institute of British Architects," 740.

63. "The late Mr. Richardson," 141.

64. James Fergusson and Robert Kerr, *History of the Modern Styles of Architecture* (London, 1891), 357–358.

65. "American architecture, *British Architect*, XXXI (January 18, 1889), 47.

66. Horace Townsend, "The house that Jonathan builds," *Builder*, LXI (April 4, 1891), 269–270.

67. See Hinckeldeyn, "Henry H. Richardson," *Centralblatt der Bauverwaltung*, VI (June 5, 1886), 221–222.

68. "Henry Richardson und seine Bedeutung für die amerikanische Architektur," *Deutsche Bauzeitung*, XXVI (February 6, 1892), 64–66.

69. "Bibliothèque publique à Malden, Mass.," 46–47.

70. "The *American Architect*," *British Architect*, XXV (February 12, 1886), 157.

71. See "Austin Hall, Harvard Law Schools, Cambridge, Mass." *Builder*, IL (December 19, 1885), 858, and "Public library, Woburn, Mass.," *Architect*, XXXV (June 25, 1886), 389.

72. Jacques Hermant, "L'architecture aux États-Unis et a l'exposition universelle de Chicago," *L'Architecture*, VII (October 20, 1894), 343.

I. 1   W. Thornton and others, T. U. Walter and E. Clark; UNITED STATES CAPITOL, Washington, D.C., 1792–1828 (central section) and 1851–1865 (wings and dome).

I. 2   R. M. Upjohn; Connecticut State Capitol, Hartford, Ct. 1872–1878.

I. 3  A. B. Mullett; State, War and Navy Building, Washington, D.C., 1871–1887.

I. 4  H. H. Richardson; Oakes Ames Memorial Town Hall, North Easton, Mass., 1879–1881.

I. 5 Peabody and Stearns; Crowe Memorial Museum of Fine Arts, St. Louis, Mo., 1879–1881.

I. 6 Sturgis and Brigham; Museum of Fine Arts, Boston, Mass., 1870–1876.

I. 7 Fernbach and de Lemos; Eden Musée, New York, N.Y., c. 1883.

I. 8  H. H. Richardson; Winn Memorial Library, Woburn, Mass., 1877–1878.

I. 9  H. H. Richardson; Austin Hall, Harvard University, Cambridge, Mass., 1881–1883.

I. 18. C. C. Haight: Hamilton Hall, Columbia University, New York, N.Y., 1880.

I. 11  G. B. Post; Produce Exchange, New York, N.Y., 1881–1885.

I. 12  Kimball and Wisedell; Entrance to the Casino Theater, New York, N.Y., 1880–1882.

I. 13   Peabody and Stearns; Church of the Messiah, St. Louis, Mo., 1880.

I. 14 H. H. Richardson; Trinity Church, Boston, Mass., 1872–1877.

I. 15  E. T. Potter; Church of the Good Shepherd, Hartford, Ct., 1868.

**I.** 16  A. Fehmer; Allyn Memorial, Spring Grove Cemetery, Hartford, Ct., 1882–1883.

I. 17    L. Eidlitz; Temple Emanu-El, New York, N.Y., 1866–1868.

I. 18    H. H. Richardson; Trinity Church Rectory, Boston, Mass., 1879.

**I.** 19    E. F. Baldwin; Central Offices of the Baltimore and Ohio Railroad,
Baltimore, Md., 1880–1882.

**I.** 20    Clinton and Pirsson; Queens Insurance Company, New York, N.Y., 1877.

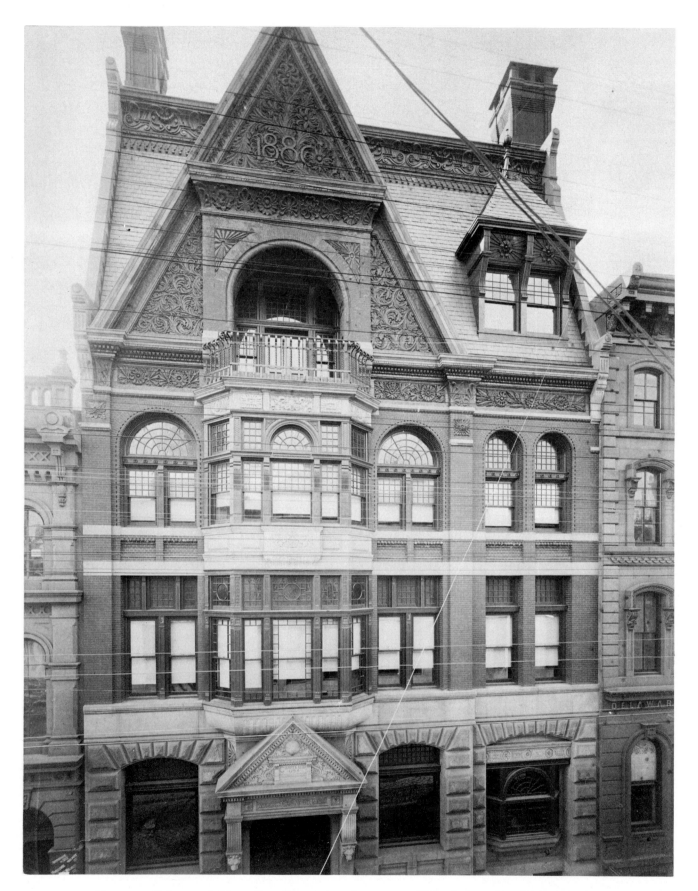

I. 21    Cabot and Chandler; Insurance Company of North America, Philadelphia, Pa., 1880.

I. 22    T. P. Chandler; Liverpool, London and Globe Insurance Company,
Philadelphia, Pa., c. 1882.

I. 23    G. B. Post; Mills Building, New York, N.Y., 1881–1883.

I. 24    Burnham and Root; National Bank of Illinois, Chicago, Ill., 1885.

I. 25    J. J. Flanders; J. B. Mallers Building, Chicago, Ill., 1884–1885.

I. 26    Burnham and Root; Insurance Exchange, Chicago, Ill., 1884–1885.

I. 27  H. H. Richardson; Detail of the Cheney Block, Hartford, Ct., 1875–1876.

**I.** 28    W. H. Dennis; Office Building, Minneapolis, Minn.

I. 29    W. W. Smith; Sloane Store, New York, N.Y., 1881.

I. 30    Peabody and Stearns; R. H. White Store, Boston, Mass. 1877.

**I.** 31    Ogden and Wright; John G. Myers Store, Albany, N.Y., c. 1884.

I. 32    Cook and Babb: Warehouse, New York, N.Y., c. 1880.

I. 33    C. L. Carson; Commercial Buildings, Baltimore, Md., 1881 and 1883.

I. 34    C. L. Carson; Commercial Building, Baltimore, Md.

I. 35    C. L. Carson; Ambach, Burgunder and Company, Baltimore, Md., 1882.

I. 36   Commercial Building, Milwaukee, Wis., 1881.

**I.** 37   Gaither Buildings, Baltimore, Md.

I. 38   Hartwell and Richardson; Odd Fellows Hall, Cambridge, Mass., 1884.

**I.** 39   Adler and Sullivan; Rothschild Store, Chicago, Ill., 1880–1881.

I. 40   J. M. Slade; Office Building, New York, N.Y., 1880.

II. I  Herter Brothers; William H. Vanderbilt Residence, New York, N.Y., 1880–1884.

**II.** 2    Herter Brothers; Detail of the William H. Vanderbilt Residence, New York, N.Y., 1880–1884.

**II.** 3    G. B. Post; Detail of the Cornelius Vanderbilt Residence, New York, N.Y., 1879–1882.

II. 4    G. B. Post; Cornelius Vanderbilt Residence, New York, N.Y., 1879–1882.

II. 5    G. B. Post; Cornelius Vanderbilt Residence, New York, N.Y., 1879–1882.

il. 6  R. M. Hunt; Detail of the William K. Vanderbilt Residence, New York, N.Y., 1879–1881.

II. 7    C. Vaux; Governor Samuel J. Tilden Residence, New York, N.Y., 1872–
1874.

II. 8    E. H. Kendall; Ogden Goelet Residence, New York, N.Y., c. 1882.

II. 9   C. B. Atwood; Dr. Stewart Webb and H. McKinley Twombly Residences, New York, N.Y., c. 1885.

II. 10  Peabody and Stearns; John C. Phillips Residence, Boston, Mass., 1877–1879.

**II.** 11  J. H. Besarick; Detail of the James Converse Residence, Boston, Mass.,
1884.

II. 12   C. Fehmer; Detail of the Oliver Ames Residence, Boston, Mass., 1882.

**II.** 13  Burnham and Root; Augustus Byram Residence, Chicago, Ill.

II. 14   Allen and Kenway; M. Washburn Residence, Boston, Mass., 1880.

II. 16   Wheelock and Clay; Private Residence, Chicago, Ill.

II. 17  Wheelock and Clay; Private Residences, Chicago, Ill.

**II.** 18    F. K. Schock; Private Residence, Chicago, Ill.

II. 19    S. Hannaford; John E. Bell Residence, Cincinnati, O., 1881–1882.

**Il. 20** C. C. Nichols; Private Residence, Albany, N.Y.

II. 21    W. Scott and Company; Simon J. Murphy Residence, Detroit, Mich.

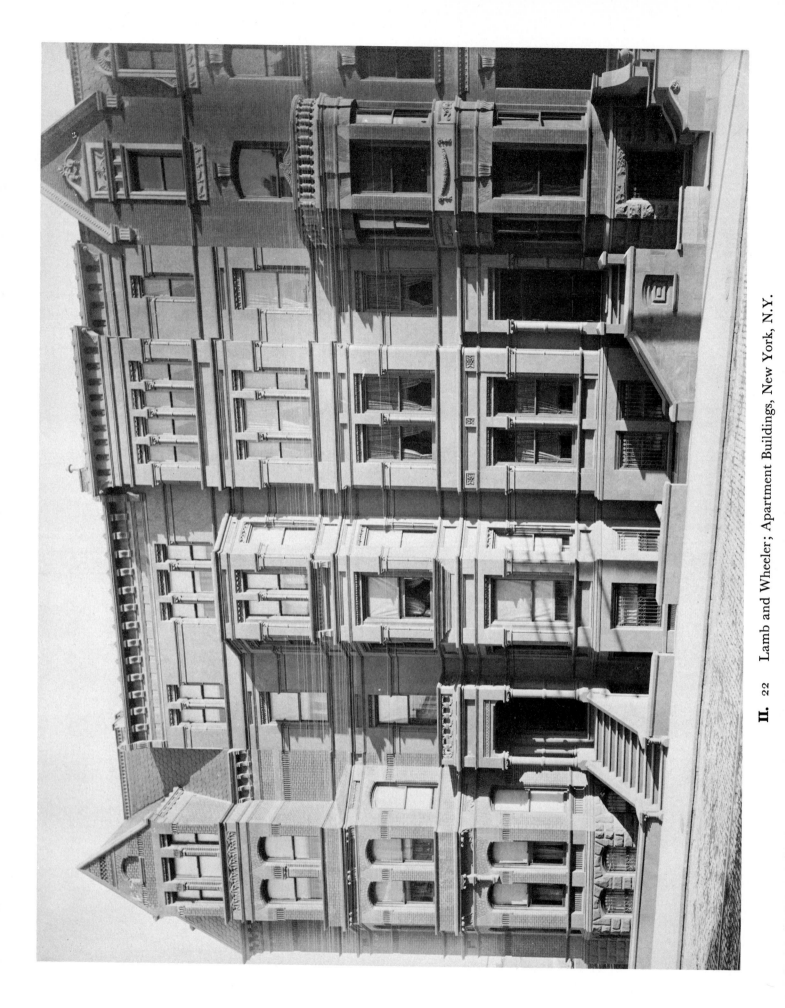

II. 22   Lamb and Wheeler; Apartment Buildings, New York, N.Y.

**II.** 23    R. H. Robertson; Private Residence, New York, N.Y., 1881.

II. 24   Apartment Buildings, New York, N.Y.

II. 25    Cabot and Chandler; Private Residence, Boston, Mass., 1880.

**II.** 26   Kirby and Lewis; Horace Billings and H. Tuttle Residences, Boston, Mass., 1879.

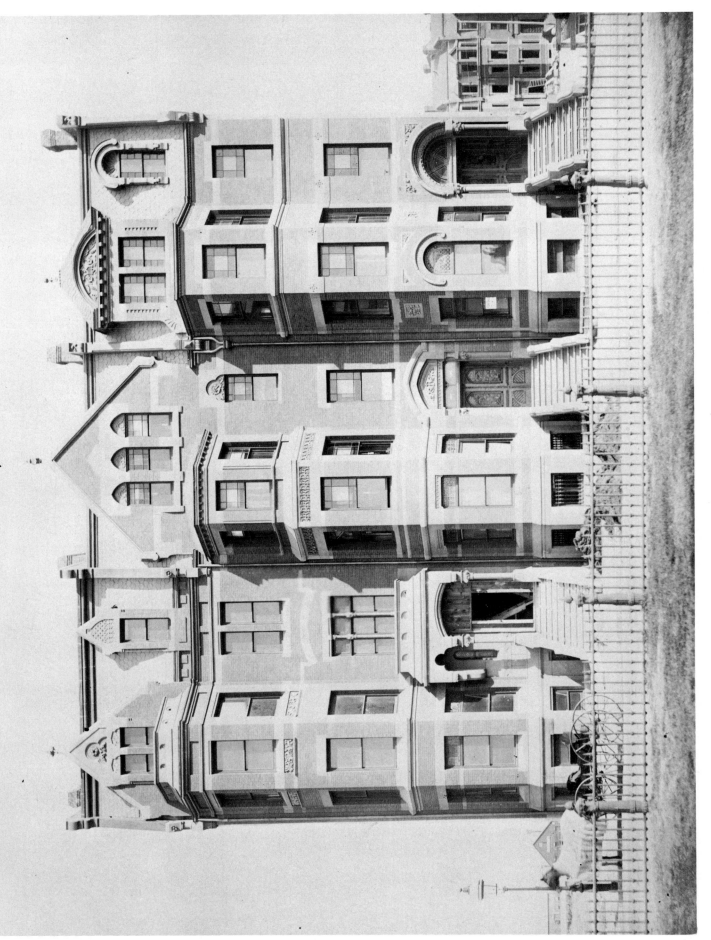

Ⅱ. 27   Kirby and Lewis; Private Residences, Boston, Mass., 1880.

II. 28   Private Residences, Washington, D.C.

II. 29    C. Pfeifer, "The Berkshires," New York, N.Y., 1883–1884.

II. 30 Peabody and Stearns, Vestibule of the J. H. White Residence, Brookline, Mass., 1880–1881.

II. 31   W. R. Emerson; Vestibule of a Summer Residence, North East Harbor, Me.

II. 32    W. R. Emerson; Vestibule of a Summer Residence, North East Harbor, Me.

II. 33   L. T. Schofield; Dining-room Buffet, Cleveland, O.

Il. 34  Burling and Whitehouse (architects), A. Fiedler (decorator); Dining Room of the S. M. Nickerson Residence, Chicago, Ill., 1883.

II. 35    Burling and Whitehouse (architects), A. Fiedler (decorator); Smoking
Room of the S. M. Nickerson Residence, Chicago, Ill., 1883.

II. 36    H. H. Richardson; Fireplace of the Oakes Ames Memorial Library, North Easton, Mass., 1877.

II. 37    Peabody and Stearns; Fireplace of the Ladies' Parlor of the R. H. White
Store, Boston, Mass. 1881.

II. 38   H. J. Schwartzmann and Company; Music Room and Conservatory, New York, N.Y.

II. 39   Burling and Whitehouse (architects), A. Fiedler (decorator); Bedroom of the S. M. Nickerson Residence, Chicago, Ill., 1883.

**II.** 40   G. W. Lloyd; Bar Room, Detroit, Mich.

III. 1   C. K. Garrison; C. K. Garrison Residence, Elberon, N. J., 1881-1882.

III. 2    McKim, Mead and White; Charles G. Francklyn Residence, Elberon, N.J., c. 1876.

III. 3　V. C. Taylor; Thomas T. Kinney Residence, Elberon, N.J., 1881.

III. 4  G. B. Post; "Château-Nooga," C. C. Baldwin Residence, Newport, R.I., 1880–1881

III. 5 Peabody and Stearns; "Vinland," Catherine Lorillard Wolfe Residence, Newport, R.I., 1882–1884.

III. 6 Rotch and Tilden; "Chatwold," Mrs. G. B. Bowler Residence, Bar Harbor, Me., c. 1883.

**III.** 7  Rotch and Tilden; Detail of "Chatwold," Mrs. G. B. Bowler Residence, Bar Harbor, Me., c. 1883.

III. 8   P. G. Boticher; Private Residence, Orange, N.J.

Ill. 9   A. H. Dodd; Private Residence, Orange, N.J.

III. 10 Private Residence, Orange, N.J.

III. 11  H. H. Holly; Henry C. Pedder Residence, Llewellyn Park, Orange, N.J.

III. 12  George Keller: Antoinette Phelps Residence, Hartford, Ct., c. 1880.

III. 13  F. C. Withers; Dr. G. Pierrepont Davis Residence, Hartford, Ct. 1881.

III. 14 Kimball and Wisedell; Franklin Chamberlin Residence, Hartford, Ct., 1881–1884.

III. 15   Row Houses, Hartford, Ct.

III. 16   C. S. Luce; Edward Stanwood Residence, Brookline, Mass., 1880.

III. 17    Peabody and Stearns; Joseph H. White Residence, Brookline, Mass., 1880–1881.

III. 18   S. E. Toby; Private Residence, Brookline, Mass.

III. 19  S. E. Toby; Private Residence, Brookline, Mass.

Ill. 20   E. A. P. Newcomb; Private Residence, Brookline, Mass.

III. 21  W. R. Emerson; J. Greenough Residence, Jamaica Plain, Mass., 1880.

III. 22   W. R. Emerson; Private Residence, Jamaica Plain, Mass.

Ill. 23 Mason and Rice; Private Residence, Detroit, Mich.

Ill. 24   W. Scott and Company; Private Residence, Detroit, Mich.

III. 25   J. L. Silsbee; Private Residence, Buffalo, N.Y.

III. 26 J. L. Silsbee; Private Residence, Buffalo, N.Y.

III. 27    J. L. Silsbee; Private Residence, Buffalo, N.Y.

Ill. 28    Cobb and Frost; Private Residence, Chicago, Ill.

III. 29   J. J. Flanders; Private Residence, Chicago, Ill.

Ill. 30 Cabot and Chandler; Elbridge Torrey Residence, Dorchester, Mass., 1880.

Ill. 31   M. A. Roberts; Charles L. Colby Residence, Milwaukee, Wisc.

III. 32 Peabody and Stearns; Charles W. Bingham Residence, Cleveland, O.

Ill. 33   J. G. Cutler; Private Residence, Rochester, N.Y.

Ill. 34  B. Price; J. M. Wayne Neff Residence, Cincinnati, O., 1881.

**III.** 35    Wheelock and Clay; M. D. Wells Residence, Chicago, Ill., c. 1884.

Ill. 36    Peabody and Stearns; Lambert Tree Residence, Chicago, Ill., 1883–1884.

III. 37   Wheelock and Clay; Private Residences, Chicago, Ill.

Ill. 38   H. H. Richardson; F. L. Ames Gate Lodge, North Easton, Mass., 1880.

III. 39   H. H. Richardson; F. L. Ames Gate Lodge, North Easton, Mass., 1880.

III. 40 Peabody and Stearns; Catherine Lorillard Wolfe Gate Lodge, "Vinland," Newport, R.I., 1882–1884.

# NOTES ON THE PLATES

## INTRODUCTION

THE PURPOSE OF THESE NOTES is two-fold: to summarize statistically the material represented in this collection and to share information discovered in attempting to document these examples of late nineteenth-century American architecture. Since the list of locations and architects included with the original publication was incomplete and, in a few instances, inaccurate, it has been necessary to supplement this basic information. Because it has been impossible to determine when certain buildings were constructed, for whom and by whom they were designed, and whether they are still standing, not all the photographs are discussed. In general, the notes contain summarized information about the architects, a discussion of problems in documentation, a bibliography for late nineteenth-century American and European references and recently published scholarship on these buildings. The references are not presumed to be complete but are included as a guide to further research.

On the most general level, the French saw American architecture as being primarily an urban phenomenon—the first two sections of *L'Architecture Américaine* were entirely devoted to city buildings. Even the third section, supposedly showing suburban and resort houses, contains row houses and other examples from major urban centers. The selection emphasizes the strong French interest in

American domestic architecture, represented by the second and third sections. Bearing in mind this imbalance in favor of domestic design, it is interesting to note what types of buildings the French did and did not choose to include. Among forty examples of public architecture, twenty-three buildings are commercial structures. Of the remaining seventeen examples of public architecture, five are for religious purposes, four are governmental buildings, three are for education and three are for art, one is a monument, and one is a theater. Landscape is completely avoided—no parks, cemeteries, streets, or squares are included. Railroad stations, hospitals, primary and secondary schools, bridges, prisons, and exhibition buildings are omitted. The lone apartment building and eight photographs of rowhouses or contiguous dwellings among the seventy domestic examples show the French fascination for the free-standing American residence.

Geographically, less than one quarter of the country is included in this selection. The breakdown, according to the number of buildings included in *L'Architecture Américaine*, is as follows:

| | |
|---|---|
| NEW YORK CITY | 21 |
| CHICAGO | 15 |
| BOSTON | 12 |
| HARTFORD | 8 |
| BALTIMORE | 5 |

| | |
|---|---|
| BROOKLINE, MASS. | 5 |
| DETROIT | 4 |
| ORANGE, N.J. | 4 |
| ELBERON, N.J. | 3 |
| NEWPORT | 3 |
| NORTH EASTON, MASS. | 3 |
| WASHINGTON | 3 |
| ALBANY | 2 |
| BUFFALO | 2 |
| CAMBRIDGE, MASS. | 2 |
| CINCINNATI | 2 |
| CLEVELAND | 2 |
| JAMAICA PLAIN, MASS. | 2 |
| MILWAUKEE | 2 |
| PHILADELPHIA | 2 |
| ST. LOUIS | 2 |
| BAR HARBOR, ME. | 1 |
| DORCHESTER, MASS. | 1 |
| MINNEAPOLIS | 1 |
| NORTH EAST HARBOR, ME. | 1 |
| ROCHESTER | 1 |
| WOBURN, MASS. | 1 |

Although an obvious attempt was made to provide some sort of national representation, the token attention paid to cities such as Minneapolis, Milwaukee, St. Louis, Cincinnati, and Cleveland only further emphasizes the strong Eastern orientation. Within this urban bias, three cities emerge as the absolute leaders of the United States architecturally—New York, Chicago, and Boston. Together they represent more than one third of all the examples chosen. More revealing, however, is the number of projects executed by architectural firms located in these three cities. Boston architects were responsible for thirty-six structures, within and outside of that city; New York firms planned twenty-seven of the buildings included; Chicago architects fifteen. Many of these firms or architects were active far from their home offices. For example, Peabody and Stearns, the most widely illustrated firm in the collection, executed more commissions outside the Boston area than it did within it. In all, approximately two-thirds of the one hundred and ten buildings were executed by architects from these three cities.

A chronological analysis of *L'Architecture Américaine* also provides several insights into the building profession in the United States. Among the examples of public architecture, more than one third of the buildings chosen were constructed before 1880, suggesting that the French saw a somewhat established tradition of public design in this new country. At the same time, some of the commercial structures, especially those in Chicago, are among the latest buildings in the survey. Most of the examples of urban domestic architecture center around the year 1880. The third group, however, is composed of predominantly post 1880 buildings, perhaps indicating a recent rise of suburban and resort architecture in this country.

During the year prior to the publication of *L'Architec-*

*ture Américaine,* the *American Architect and Building News* (June 13, 1885, pp. 282–283) conducted a poll of its readers to determine the best examples of architecture in the United States. The results were rather disappointing; only seventy-five readers responded, thirty-one of whom were from four cities—New York, Boston, Philadelphia, and Chicago. One hundred and seventy-five buildings were nominated with fifty-six receiving more than one vote. Eight of the top twenty buildings chosen in this poll were also included in *L'Architecture Américaine.* Overall, however, only fourteen buildings in the poll were selected for the French publication. Of the best twenty buildings chosen, seven were in New York, four in Boston, and none in Chicago. All but one of the twenty structures were examples of public architecture. American architects participating in the poll apparently felt that their best work was in the field of public architecture (the self-conscious nature of the poll may have influenced them to select the largest buildings of public function). The French critics, however, were interested primarily in American domestic designs.

Although André, Daly Fils et C$^{ie}$ were either unaware of, or not strongly influenced by this poll, a great many of the buildings in *L'Architecture Américaine* were probably chosen because they had been published in American books or architectural journals. The most important organ of the architectural profession in the United States and the most valuable source of illustrations abroad at that time was the *American Architect and Building News,* first published in 1876. The French were definitely aware of this publication and relied upon it almost exclusively in forming their impression of the development of architecture in North America. The strong Eastern bias of this magazine may account, to a degree, for the domination of Eastern examples in *L'Architecture Américaine.* Two other sources to which the French could have turned in making their selection were the *Inland Architect and News Record,* which began publication in Chicago in 1883, and *Artistic Houses, being a series of interior views of the most beautiful and celebrated homes in the United States . . .,* issued by the Appleton publishing house in 1883–1884. At least forty-three of the one hundred and twenty photographs of buildings and interiors in *L'Architecture Américaine* were published with an illustration or description in one of these three sources before 1886. Many others were certainly listed in the news of construction in various cities. Although forty-three buildings had been published in American books and periodicals, none of the photographs in *L'Architecture Américaine* are, to my knowledge, copies of published photographs.

How was the collection of photographs that comprises *L'Architecture Américaine* formed? We have no information about the number of photographers, whether they were American or French, or when they did their work. However, certain facts can be learned from the photographs themselves. It can be definitely proven that the photographs were taken over a period of several years. The Vanderbilt houses (Pls. II.1–6) in New York City were photographed before they were completed. All three buildings were under construction in 1881. The National Bank of Illinois (Pl. I.24) was not erected until 1885, a year before the publication of *L'Architecture Américaine*. Thus, the photography was not completed in one grand tour of the United States. Also, this series of photographs appears to be the work of several men of varying talent. For example, the photographs of the two buildings from Philadelphia (Pl. I.21, 22) are vastly inferior to the general quality of the photographs taken in New York or Boston. Here, the buildings are distorted, the top and bottom cut out of the photograph, and part of the building hidden in deep shadow. By comparing either of these Philadelphia examples with a typical New York photograph (Pl. I.10), it is immediately obvious that at least two photographers were involved with the project. The New York photographer carefully chose his composition—including a bit of a building to the left, giving depth to the photograph, a corner angle and some of the surroundings—and waited for perfect light conditions. On a purely practical level, it is more logical to asssume that the publishers gathered the work of several photographers rather than commissioning one man to visit one hundred and ten sites. One can only speculate, however, about the exact number of photographers involved.

What has happended to these buildings that were chosen by the French in 1886 as being worthy of study? Out of seventy-nine known instances, only thirty-five buildings are standing today. It is also unlikely that many of the unidentified buildings are still extant. Boston, which ranked third with twelve buildings in 1886, has lost only two in the intervening years. Hartford has also saved most of the buildings that the French admired. Other cities—such as Philadelphia, Baltimore, and Cincinnati—have torn down all the buildings included in this survey. That so few of these buildings are still standing emphasizes the importance of republishing *L'Architecture Américaine*. Few copies of this volume exist today, making it unavailable to a general audience. The wide range of buildings and interiors representing notable and curious examples of American architecture, make this rare survey an unusual document of its time. *L'Architecture Américaine* represents true history, not flavored by the prejudices and influences of today.

I should like to mention briefly those who assisted in the documentation of these buildings. For all the references to American buildings in European books and periodicals, I am indebted to Arnold Lewis. For helping to identify buildings in certain cities or by particular architects, I should like to thank: James F. Durnell for Elberon, N.J.; M. W. Jacobus for Hartford, Ct.; David Kiehl for New York City; Wheaton Holden for Peabody and Stearns; and Cynthia Zaitzevsky for William Ralph Emerson.

# NOTES

PLATE I.1: *United States Capitol, Washington, D.C.; central section 1792–1828 (William Thornton and others); wings and dome 1851–1865 (Thomas U. Walter and Edward Clark); standing.*

The French were specifically interested in the changes on the Capitol brought about by Thomas Ustick Walter (1804–1887) and Edward Clark (1827–1902), the fourth and fifth architects of the Capitol, respectively. Walter designed the cast-iron dome and the wings added to the north and south facades. Clark completed many of the projects begun by Walter and employed Frederick Law Olmsted to landscape part of the Capitol grounds. In 1885 the American architectural profession designated the United States Capitol the second best building in the country: "The best ten buildings in the United States." *American Architect and Building News*, XVII (June 13, 1885), 282.

In general, the Europeans were critical of the Capitol's cast-iron dome, considering it an example of architectural deceit. The following articles by French, English, and German critics present the variations of the European point of view:

"The architectural employment of iron." *Architect*, XXXI (March 22, 1884), 185.
"The arts in a new country." *Architect*, XVIII (December 15, 1877), 321.
"Das Capitol zu Washington." *Wochenblatt für Baukunde*, IX (January 28, 1887), 41–42.

Fergusson, James. *History of the Modern Styles of Architecture.* 2nd ed. London: John Murray, 1873, 498–512.
Hinckeldeyn, C. "A foreigner's view of American architecture." *American Architect and Building News*, XXV (May 25, 1889), 243.
"Les nouveaux capitoles aux États-Unis." *La Semaine des Constructeurs*, III (March 22, 1879), 452.
Planat, P. "Modern architecture." *American Architect and Building News*, XXXVII (August 20, 1892), 111–113. This article was reprinted from: *Encyclopédie de l'Architecture et de la Construction*, 1st ed. Vol V, 723–724.

For a good discussion of the work of Walter and Clark on the Capitol see: Mario E. Campioli, "Thomas U. Walter, Edward Clark, and the United States Capitol," *Journal of the Society of Architectural Historians*, XXIII (December, 1964), 210–213.

PLATE I.2: *Connecticut State Capitol, Hartford, Ct.; 1872–1878; Richard M. Upjohn; standing.*

Richard M. Upjohn (1827–1903) was the son of Richard Upjohn, the noted architect of Trinity Church, New York City. In the 1885 *American Architect* poll of the ten best buildings in the country, R. M. Upjohn's Connecticut State Capitol was rated number six: "The best ten buildings in the United States." *American Architect and Building News*, XVII (June 13, 1885), 282. This building was also published in: "The

Connecticut State Capitol, Hartford, Ct." *American Architect and Building News*, VII (June 19, 1880), 54.

Foreign cities also praised the Connecticut State Capitol. Karl Hinckeldeyn, the German critic, considered this building to be superior to both the Philadelphia City Hall and the New York State Capitol although he found it lacking in monumentality: C. Hinckeldeyn, "A foreigner's view of American architecture." *American Architect and Building News*, XXV (May 25, 1889), 243.

The reactions of other European critics included:

Planat, P. "Architecture moderne." *Encylcopédie de l'Architecture et de la Construction.* 1st ed. Vol. V, 723–724.
Sgt., W. "Das Kapitol zu Washington." *Deutsche Bauzeitung*, XXI (May 7, 1887), 217–218.
Soissons, S. C. de. *A Parisian in America.* Boston: Estes and Laurait, 1896, 161–162.

PLATE I.3: *State, War and Navy Building, Washington, D.C.; 1871–1887; Alfred B. Mullett; standing.*

Alfred B. Mullett (1834–1890) was appointed Supervising Architect of the Treasury Building in 1866. While holding this office, he designed major public buildings in the Second Empire style for New York City, Philadelphia, St. Louis, and Cincinnati, in addition to the State, War and Navy Building in Washington. For further information see: Lawrence Wodehouse, "Alfred B. Mullett and his French style government buildings," *Journal of the Society of Architectural Historians*, XXXI (March, 1972), 22–37.

One of the few European critics to mention A. B. Mullett was William Fogerty (1834–1878), an Irish architect who had practiced in the United States for approximately three years in the early seventies. He referred to Mullett in an address before the Royal Institute of Irish Architects, April 15, 1875. Fogerty saw Mullett as the source for a new national style which he entitled "American Renaissance." He also used Mullett as an example of how American architects received embarrassingly low salaries.

"Ayrtonism in America." *Architect*, XVI (July 1, 1876), 3–4.
Fogerty, W. "On the conditions and practices of architecture in the United States." *Practical Magazine*, new ser. VI (1876), 82.

PLATE I.4: *Oakes Ames Memorial Town Hall, North Easton, Mass.; 1879–1881; H. H. Richardson; standing.*

Widely admired in America and abroad, the Oakes Ames Memorial Town Hall was constructed on a picturesque site that was later improved by Frederick Law Olmsted. The building was the second public structure in North Easton commissioned by the Ames family. The Oliver Ames Memorial Library, visible in the right corner of the photograph, was designed by Richardson in 1877. He also received commissions for a train station and a gate lodge (Pls. III.38, 39) for the Ames family in North Easton. In the 1885 *American Architect* poll, the North Easton Town Hall was rated the tenth best building in the country. The building was also included in an exhibition at the Royal Institute of British Architects in March, 1886, arranged by J. B. Gass, the second Godwin Bursary holder to visit this country.

"The best ten buildings in the United States." *American Architect and Building News*, XVII (June 13, 1885), 282.

Hitchcock, Henry-Russell. *The Architecture of H. H. Richardson and His Times.* Revised ed. Cambridge: The M.I.T. Press, 1961, 185, 197–199.
"The late Mr. Richardson." *Royal Institute of British Architects, Journal of Proceedings*, new ser. IV (February 9, 1888), 141.
"Modern American architecture." *British Architect*, XIX (January 5, 1883), 7 and (March 30, 1883), 154–155.
"Some American methods." *Royal Institute of British Architects. Journal of Proceedings*, new ser. II (1886), 161–162.
"Town Hall, North Easton, Mass." *American Architect and Building News*, XIII (May 10, 1883), 235.
Townsend, Horace. "H. H. Richardson, architect." *Magazine of Art*, (1894), 137.
Van Rensselaer, Mariana Griswold. *Henry Hobson Richardson and His Works.* New York: Dover Publications, 1969, 71–72.

PLATE I.5: *Crowe Memorial Museum of Fine Arts, corner of 19th and Locust streets, St. Louis, Mo.; 1879–1881; Peabody and Stearns; destroyed.*

Robert Swain Peabody (1845–1917) and Charles Goddard Stearns (1843–1917) were the senior partners of the best architectural firm in the United States—according to the representation of their works in *L'Architecture Américaine*. The success of the museum project encouraged Peabody and Stearns to establish a permanent office in St. Louis which later handled the commission for the Church of the Messiah (Fig. I.13).

The Crowe Memorial Museum of Fine Arts consisted of two large exhibition galleries on either side of the central entrance hall and an auditorium extending at right angles behind the main section shown in the photograph.

"Museum of Fine Arts, St. Louis, Mo., Messrs Peabody and Stearns, Architects, Boston, Mass." *American Architect and Building News*, X (September 3, 1881), 111.
Holden, Wheaton Arnold. "Robert Swain Peabody of Peabody and Stearns in Boston—The Early Years (1870–1886)." Unpublished Ph.D. dissertation, Boston University, 1969, 120–122.
————. "The Peabody Touch: Peabody and Stearns of Boston, 1870–1917." *Journal of the Society of Architectural Historians*, XXXII (May, 1973), 118.

PLATE I.6: *Museum of Fine Arts, Copley Square, Boston Mass.; 1870–1876; Sturgis and Brigham; destroyed.*

*American Architect and Building News*, VIII (October 30, 1880), 205–206.
"The City of Boston." *Engineering*, VL (June 29, 1888), 623.
Floyd, Margaret Henderson. "A Terra-Cotta Cornerstone for Copley Square: Museum of Fine Arts, Boston, 1870–1876, by Sturgis and Brigham." *Journal of the Society of Architectural Historians*, XXXII (May, 1973), 83–103.

PLATE I.7: *Eden Musée, 55 West 23rd Street, New York, N.Y.; c. 1883; H. Fernbach and T. de Lemos; destroyed.*

The Eden Musée was the first New York commission of Theodore de Lemos (1850–1909) and the final project of Henry Fernbach (1828–1883). Since Fernbach died before the building was completed, the Eden Musée can be roughly dated 1883. Fernbach was also involved with Leopold Eidlitz in the commission for Temple Emanu-El (Pl. I.17).

PLATE I.8: *Winn Memorial Library, Woburn, Mass.; 1877–1878; H. H. Richardson; standing.*

The Winn Memorial Library was one of the earliest in a long series of town libraries designed by Henry Richardson. The building was included in the exhibition of American architecture given at the R.I.B.A. in March, 1886, by John B. Gass.

*American Architect and Building News*, II (March 3, 1877), 68.
Fergusson, James and Kerr, Robert. *History of the Modern Styles of Architecture.* 3rd ed. London: John Murray, 1891, II, 360–361.
"Public Library, Woburn, Mass." *Architect*, XXXV (June 25, 1886), 389.

PLATE I.9: *Austin Hall, Harvard University, Cambridge, Mass.; 1881–1883; H. H. Richardson; standing.*

Austin Hall, built for the Harvard Law School, was included in J. B. Gass' R.I.B.A. exhibition in 1886. It was Richardson's Sever Hall at Harvard, however, rather than Austin Hall, that was chosen by the 1885 poll in the *American Architect and Building News.*

In European architectural journals, Austin Hall was the second most commonly illustrated or mentioned Richardson building, preceded only by Trinity Church (Pl. I.14).

"Austin Hall, Cambridge, Mass." *American Architect and Building News*, XVII (March 28, 1885), 151.
"Austin Hall, Harvard Law Schools, Cambridge, Mass." *Builder*, IL (December 19, 1885), 858.
"The best ten buildings in the United States." *American Architect and Building News*, XVII (June 13, 1885), 282.
Graef, Paul and Hinckeldeyn, Karl. *Neubauten in Nordamerika.* Berlin: Julius Becker, 1897, plate 110.
"The late Mr. Richardson." *Royal Institute of British Architects, Journal of Proceedings*, new ser. IV (February 9, 1888), 141.
"Some American methods." *Royal Institute of British Architects, Journal of Proceedings*, new ser. II (1886), 161–162.
Townsend, Horace. "English and Amercian architecture—a comparison and a prophecy." *Art Journal*, LIV (October, 1892) 298.
Townsend, Horace. "H. H. Richardson, architect." *Magazine of Art*, (1894), 133–138.
"Université de Harvard à Cambridge, près de Boston." *Le Moniteur des Architectes*, new ser. XX (1886), 96.

PLATE I.10: *Hamilton Hall, Columbia University, New York, N.Y.; 1880; Charles C. Haight; destroyed.*

Charles Coolidge Haight (1841–1917) designed several buildings for the old campus of Columbia University, located between Madison and Park avenues and 49th and 50th streets. In addition to Hamilton Hall, which served as a dormitory, Haight was the architect for the School of Mines (1874) and the library (1884) which can be seen to the right of Hamilton Hall in the photograph. McKim, Mead and White's Villard Houses can be seen under construction at the left side of the photograph. Hamilton Hall was ranked fifteenth in the 1885 *American Architect* poll.

"The best ten buildings in the United States." *American Architect and Building News*, XVII (June 13, 1885), 282.

Schuyler, Montgomery. *American Architecture and Other Writings.* Edited by William Jordy and Ralph Coe. Cambridge: The Belknap Press of the Harvard University Press, 1961, 160n.
———. "The Works of Charles C. Haight." Great American Architects series, No. 6, *Architectural Record* (July, 1899).

PLATE I.11: *Produce Exchange, Broadway and Whitehall Street, New York, N.Y.; 1881–1885; George B. Post; destroyed.*

George Browne Post (1837–1913) won the commission for the Produce Exchange over competition drawings by R. M. Upjohn, F. C. Withers, and Leopold Eidlitz. The eight-story structure included a main trading room of 32,000 unencumbered square feet and three hundred offices. This photograph was probably taken in 1885 since the building is nearly completed except for the boarded-over doors. In 1885, the readers of *American Architect* voted the Produce Exchange the fourteenth best building in the country.

*American Architect and Building News*, XIX (June 26, 1886), 305–306.
"The best ten buildings in the United States." *American Architect and Building News*, XVII (June 13, 1885), 282.
Hinckeldeyn, C. "A foreigner's view of American architecture." *American Architect and Building News*, XXV (May 25, 1889), 244.
"The New York Produce Exchange." *Architect*, XXXI (March 22, 1884), 191.
Weisman, Winston. "The Commercial Architecture of G. B. Post." *Journal of the Society of Architectural Historians*, XXXI (October, 1972), 188–190.

PLATE I.12: *Casino Theater, northwest corner of Broadway and 39th Street, New York, N.Y.; 1880–1882; F. H. Kimball and T. Wisedell; destroyed.*

In 1879, Francis Hatch Kimball (1845–1919) and Thomas Wisedell (d. 1884) formed their partnership and were commissioned to remodel the Madison Square Theater. The success of this project brought the firm commissions for several other New York theaters, one of which was the Casino. Critics praised the firm for the fine handling of the theater's terra cotta in a Moorish design (well illustrated in the photograph). In 1881, they designed a house (Pl. III.14) in Hartford, where Kimball had worked before 1879.

*American Architect and Building News*, XVI (August 9, 1884), 61.
Hinckeldeyn, C. "A foreigner's view of American architecture." *American Architect and Building News*, XXV (May 25, 1889), 244.
Schuyler, Montgomery. *American Architecture and Other Writings.* Edited by William Jordy and Ralph Coe. Cambridge: The Belknap Press of the Harvard University Press, 1961, 97–98.
———. "The Works of Francis H. Kimball and Kimball & Thompson." *Architectural Record*, VII (April–June, 1898), 494.
Taylor, James. "The history of terra cotta in New York City." *Architectural Record*, II (1893), 143.
"Vestibule of the Casino Theater, N.Y." *Builder*, LII (April 9, 1887), 538.

PLATE I.13: *Church of the Messiah, Garrison Avenue and Locust Street, St. Louis. Mo.; 1880; Peabody and Stearns; standing.*

The Church of the Messiah, erected concurrently with the Crowe Memorial Museum of Fine Arts (Pl. I.5), was the firm's second project in St. Louis. Peabody and Stearns hired a Mr. Furber as their resident partner during this period of great activity in St. Louis.

*American Architect and Building News*, VII (April 24, 1880), 178.
Sturgis, Russell. "A critique of the works of Shepley, Rutan & Coolidge, and Peabody & Stearns." Great American Architects series, No. 3. *Architectural Record* (July, 1896), 53.

PLATE I.14: *Trinity Church, Copley Square, Boston, Mass.; 1872–1877; H. H. Richardson; standing.*

Trinity Church, located on Copley Square at right angles to the Museum of Fine Arts (Pl. I.6) by Sturgis and Brigham, was, by popular acclaim, H. H. Richardson's finest work. The architectural community in the United States judged Trinity Church the best building in the country in the 1885 poll of the *American Architect*. J. B. Gass included Trinity Church in his 1886 exhibition at the R.I.B.A. Trinity Church was more frequently illustrated and discussed in European architectural journals than any other American building of the period.

Bing, Samuel. "L'Architecture aux États-Unis." *Le Moniteur des Architectes*, new ser. X (February, 1896), 9–14.
"A Boston basilica." *Architect*, XVII (April 28, 1877), 274.
"The City of Boston." *Engineering*, VL (June 29, 1888), 641.
"A day in Boston." *Architect*, XIX (January 5, 1878), 7.
Fletcher, Banister F. "American architecture through English spectacles." *Engineering Magazine*, VII (June, 1894), 320.
Gass, John B. "American architecture and architects, with special reference to the works of the late Richard Morris Hunt and Henry Hobson Richardson." *Royal Institute of British Architects, Journal*, ser. 3, III (February 6, 1896), 232.
Hinckeldeyn, C. "A foreigner's view of American architecture." *American Architect and Building News*, XXV (May 25, 1889), 243.
————. "Henry H. Richardson." *Centralblatt der Bauverwaltung*, VI (January 5, 1886), 221.
————. "Henry Richardson und seine Bedeutung für die amerikanische Architektur." *Deutsche Bauzeitung*, XXVI (February 6, 1892), 65.
"The late Mr. Richardson." *Royal Institute of British Architects, Journal of Proceedings*, new ser. IV (February 9, 1888), 141.
Lippert, F. G. "Kirchenwesen und protestantische Kirchenbauten in Nordamerika." *Deutsche Bauzeitung*, XXVII (May 13, 1893), 233.
Osborne, C. Francis. "La construction moderne aux États-Unis." *La Construction Moderne*, III (March 3, 1888), 243.
Perry, Th. Sargeant. "Colour decoration in America." *Architect*, XVIII (October 20, 1877), 210–211.
Pfeifer, Herm. "Neu-romanischer Baustil 'Modern Romanesque' in Nordamerika." *Deutsche Bauhütte*, III (August 17, 1899), 197–199.
Soissons, S. C. de. *A Parisian in America*. Boston: Estes and Laurait, 1896, 170.
Stebbins, Theodore E. "Richardson and Trinity Church:

The Evolution of a Building." *Journal of the Society of Architectural Historians*, XXVII (December, 1968), 281–298.
Townsend, Horace. "English and American architecture—a comparison and a prophecy." *Art Journal*, LIV (October, 1892), 300.
————. "H. H. Richardson, architect." *Magazine of Art*, (1894), 135–136.
"Trinity Church, Boston." *American Architect and Building News*, II (February 3, 1877), 36.

PLATE I.15: *Church of the Good Shepherd, Hartford, Ct.; 1868; E. T. Potter; standing.*

Edward Tuckerman Potter (d. 1904) of Schenectady, N.Y., was a church architect of wide reputation. This church was commissioned by the widow of Col. Samuel Colt as a memorial to her husband and stands directly behind the Colt Rifle Manufactory in Hartford.

PLATE I.16: *Allyn Memorial, Spring Grove Cemetery, Hartford, Ct.; 1882–1883; A. Fehmer; destroyed.*

*American Architect and Building News*, XVII (May 16, 1885), 234.

PLATE I.17: *Temple Emanu-El, corner of Fifth Avenue and 43rd Street, New York, N.Y.; 1866–1868; Leopold Eidlitz; destroyed in 1927.*

Leopold Eidlitz (1823–1906) was assisted in this commission by Henry Fernbach (1829–1883), a member of the congregation of Temple Emanu-El. In attempting to create an oriental form, the architects designed a basically Gothic building with Saracenic decoration. Although not ranked among the best twenty buildings in the country, this synagogue was nominated in the 1885 *American Architect* poll.

"The best ten buildings in the United States." *American Architect and Building News*, XVII (June 13, 1885), 283.
Schuyler, Montgomery. *American Architecture and Other Writings*. Edited by William Jordy and Ralph Coe. Cambridge: The Belknap Press of the Harvard University Press, 1961, 155–157.
Wischnitzer, Rachel. *Synagogue Architecture in the United States*. Philadelphia: Jewish Publishing Society of America, 1955, 74–75.

PLATE I.18: *Trinity Church Rectory, corner of Newbury and Clarendon streets, Boston, Mass.; 1879; H. H. Richardson; standing.*

The building was commissioned by Phillips Brooks, rector of Trinity Church and a personal friend of Richardson. In 1893, the roof was raised and a third floor was added by Shepley, Rutan and Coolidge, Richardson's successors.

Bunting, Bainbridge. *Houses of Boston's Back Bay—An Architectural History 1840–1917*. Cambridge: The Belknap Press of the Harvard University Press, 1967.
Hitchcock, Henry-Russell. *The Architecture of H. H. Richardson and His Times*. Revised ed. Cambridge: The M.I.T. Press, 1961, 200–202.
Schuyler, Montgomery. "The Romanesque Revival in America." *Architectural Record*, I (1892), 152.

PLATE I.19: *Baltimore and Ohio Railroad Office, corner of Baltimore and Calvert streets, Baltimore Md.; 1880–1882; E. F. Baldwin; destroyed in 1904.*

Ephraim Francis Baldwin (1837–1916) was associated with Bruce Price (Pl. III.34) between 1867 and 1873. The original design for this building included a tower on Baltimore street which was omitted in construction. The building was visited in 1882 by the first Godwin Bursary holder, John Arthur Gale. A major fire in central Baltimore destroyed the structure in 1904.

"Central Offices of the Baltimore and Ohio Railroad Company, Baltimore, Md., Mr. E. F. Baldwin, Architect, Baltimore." *American Architect and Building News*, VIII (August 14, 1880), 73.

Hungerford, Edward. *The Story of the Baltimore and Ohio Railroad 1827–1927*. New York: G. P. Putnam's Sons, 1928, 150.

PLATE I.20: *Queens Insurance Company Building, 37 and 39 Wall Street, New York, N.Y.; 1877; C. W. Clinton and J. W. Pirsson; destroyed.*

*American Architect and Building News*, II (September 29, 1877), 313.

PLATE I.21: *Insurance Company of North America, 232 Walnut Street, Philadelphia, Pa.; 1880; Cabot and Chandler; destroyed.*

Showing the national patronage of some Boston firms, Edward Clarke Cabot (1818–1901) and Francis Chandler (1844–1925) designed this Philadelphia building. The form and decoration are very similar to a Boston house (Pl. II.25) designed by Cabot and Chandler in the same year. Although it only received two votes, the Insurance Company of North America was included in the 1885 poll of the best architecture in the United States conducted by the *American Architect*.

*American Architect and Building News*, VIII (July 31, 1880), 54.

"The ten best buildings in the United States." *American Architect and Building News*, XVII (June 13, 1885), 283.

PLATE I.22: *Liverpool, London and Globe Insurance Company, 333 Walnut Street, Philadelphia, Pa.; c. 1882; T. P. Chandler; destroyed.*

Although European interest in American architecture had begun in Philadelphia with the Centennial Celebration of 1876, Theophilus Parsons Chandler (1845–1928) was the only Philadelphia architect included in this collection of photographs. Trained in Boston, Chandler moved to Philadelphia in 1870 and probably designed this building in 1882, the year in which a competition drawing for this structure by another firm was published in the *American Architect*.

"Design for the Liverpool, London and Globe Insurance Offices, Philadelphia, Pa., Messrs. Hazelhurst and Huckle, Architects, Philadelphia, Pa." *American Architect and Building News*, XII (December 16, 1882), 291.

PLATE I.23: *Mills Building, Broad Street and Exchange Place, New York, N.Y.; 1881–1883; G. B. Post; destroyed.*

Under construction at the same time as Post's Produce Exchange (Pl. I.11), the Mills Building was the largest office building of the period in New York. The building, which used a large court for light and ventilation, received attention in foreign architectural magazines.

"American planning and construction." *Builder*, XLIV (March 10, 1883), 318.

Gmelin, L. "Architektonisches aus Nordamerika." *Deutsche Bauzeitung*, XXVIII (October 27, 1894), 532.

"Sky building in New York." *Building News*, XLV (September 7, 1883), 364.

Townsend, Horace. "English and American architecture—a comparison and a prophecy." *Art Journal*, LIV (October, 1892), 297.

"Very tall building." *Architect*, XXX (September 15, 1883); 155.

Weisman, Winston. "The Commercial Architecture of G. B. Post." *Journal of the Society of Architectural Historians*, XXXI (October, 1972), 186–187.

PLATE I.24: *National Bank of Illinois, 21–29 North Dearborn Street, Chicago, Ill.; 1885; Burnham and Root; destroyed.*

Daniel Hudson Burnham (1846–1912) and John Wellborn Root (1850–1892) were commissioned to design the Grannis Block, which was constructed on this site in 1880–1881. That building was destroyed by fire in 1885, and the National Bank of Illinois, also by Burnham and Root, was a reconstruction and enlargement on the same site.

Condit, Carl. *The Rise of the Skyscraper*. Chicago: University of Chicago Press, 1952, 78.

*Inland Architect and News Record*, X (January, 1887), 2.

Root, John Wellborn. *The Meanings of Architecture: Buildings and Writings*. Introduction by Donald Hoffmann. New York: Horizon Press, 1967, plate 30.

PLATE I.25: *J. B. Mallers Office Building, southwest corner of La Salle and Quincy streets, Chicago, Ill.; 1884–1885; J. J. Flanders; destroyed in 1920.*

Despite the limitations of a small site, John J. Flanders (1847–1914) designed a twelve-story office building that was the tallest structure in Chicago at the time of its construction. Flanders also designed a Chicago house (Pl. III.29) that was included in *L'Architecture Américaine*.

Condit, Carl W. *The Chicago School of Architecture—A History of Commercial and Public Building in the Chicago Area, 1875–1925*. Chicago: University of Chicago Press, 1964, 59.

———. *The Rise of the Skyscraper*. Chicago: University of Chicago Press, 1952, 79–80, 207.

*Inland Architect and News Record*, V (July, 1885), 94.

PLATE I.26: *Insurance Exchange, southwest corner of La Salle and Adams streets, Chicago, Ill.; 1884–1885; Burnham and Root; destroyed in 1912.*

*Inland Architect and News Record*, V (July, 1885), 94.

Monroe, Harriet. *John Wellborn Root—A Study of His Life and Work*. Park Forest, Ill.: The Prairie School Press, 1966, 139.

Root, John Wellborn. *The Meanings of Architecture: Buildings and Writings*. Introduction by Donald Hoffmann. New York: Horizon Press, 1967, plate 19.

Schuyler, Montgomery. *American Architecture and Other Writings*. Edited by William Jordy and Ralph Coe.

Cambridge: The Belknap Press of the Harvard University Press, 1961, 269–272.

PLATE I.27: *Detail of the Cheney Block, 942 Main Street, Hartford, Ct.; 1875–1876; H. H. Richardson; standing.*

Erected while Richardson was involved with the construction of Trinity Church (Pl. I.14), the Cheney Block was a commission for a seven-story commercial structure. In 1877, a proposed addition was published in the *American Architect*, but the plan was never executed. This detail of the Cheney Block shows Richardson's exciting color treatment through the use of brownstone and sandstone.

Hitchcock, Henry-Russell. *The Architecture of H. H. Richardson and His Times.* Revised edition. Cambridge: The M.I.T. Press, 1961, 164–171.

PLATE I.29: *W. and J. Sloane Store, 888 Broadway, New York, N.Y.; 1881; W. W. Smith; standing.*

The Sloane Store, by W. Wheeler Smith, is an excellent example of functional design. In discussing this building, Karl Hinckeldeyn stated:

> The purpose could scarcely have been expressed better than has been done by its architect, Mr. Wheeler Smith. In the treatment of the pillars, in the arrangement of the large light openings, in the placing of the intermediate columns of iron; in short, in the composition of the whole, as well as of the details, a true artistic spirit, confident of success, is manifested.

*American Architect and Building News*, XVIII (November 20, 1885), 258.
Hinckeldeyn, C. "A foreigner's view of American architecture." *American Architect and Building News*, XXV (May 25, 1889), 244.
Weisman, Winston. "The Commercial Architecture of G. B. Post." *Journal of the Society of Architectural Historians*, XXXI (October, 1972), 183.

PLATE I.30: *R. H. White Store, 518–538 Washington Street, Boston, Mass.; 1877; Peabody and Stearns; standing.*

This original section of the R. H. White Store was expanded by Peabody and Stearns in 1881 (see Note II.37). In addition, Peabody and Stearns designed the residence of the store's owner, Mr. Joseph H. White (Pls. II.30, II.17). The photograph shows the distortion of the wide-angle lens and the problem of movement in the street.

*American Architect and Building News*, II (May 12, 1877), 148.
*American Architect and Building News*, XIV (September 15, 1883), 127.
Davison, T. Raffles. "Rambling Sketches." *British Architect*, XXV (September 24, 1886).

PLATE I.31: *John G. Myers Store, 39–41 North Pearl Street, Albany, N.Y.; c. 1884 Ogden and Wright; standing.*

*American Architect and Building News*, XVI (October 11, 1884), 176.

PLATES I.33,34,35: *Commercial Buildings, Baltimore, Md.; c. 1881; C. L. Carson; destroyed.*

During the last quarter of the nineteenth century, Charles L. Carson (1847–1891) was one of the major architects of the

Mid-Atlantic states. As a partner of Thomas Dixon from about 1870 to 1876, he designed many public buildings and private residences in Maryland and Delaware. Carson's obituary in The Baltimore *Sun* included a list of his major commissions. Among these were Ambach, Burgunder and Company (Pl. I.35) and several that may have been for Pl. I.34: the Western National Bank; the American National Bank; Hurst, Purnell and Company; and Daniel Miller and Company. Neither Sneering and Company nor Holzman and Friedenwald (Pl. I.33) were included in the list. Plates I.33 and I.35 have definitely been destroyed.

*Baltimore City Directory.* Baltimore: John W. Woods, 1880–1884.
"Charles L. Carson, the Well-Known Architect." *The Sun* (Baltimore, Md.), December 19, 1891.

PLATE I.38: *Odd Fellows Hall, Massachusetts Avenue, Cambridge, Mass.; 1884; Hartwell and Richardson; standing.*

Henry W. Hartwell (1833–1919) and William C. Richardson (1854–1935) designed this building for commercial and private purposes. The first floor was used by businesses; the three upper floors were meeting rooms for the members of the fraternal order.

*American Architect and Building News*, XVII (May 16, 1885), 234.
Vogel, Susan Maycock. "Hartwell and Richardson: An Introduction to their Work." *Journal of the Society of Architectural Historians*, XXXII (May, 1973), 142–143.

PLATE I.39: *Rothschild Store, 210 West Monroe Street, Chicago, Ill.; 1880–1881; Adler and Sullivan; destroyed.*

The Rothschild Store was one of the first commissions executed by the partnership of Dankmar Adler (1844–1900) and Louis Sullivan (1856–1924). It is surprising that this building was included in *L'Architecture Américaine* since European critics had taken little notice of the young firm.

Morrison, Hugh. *Louis Sullivan—Prophet of Modern Architecture.* New York: W. W. Norton and Company, 1935, 58–59.

PLATE I.40: *Office Building, 753 Broadway, New York, N.Y.; 1880; J. M. Slade; destroyed.*

Although he had been apprenticed to Edward Kendell (Pl. II.8), who specialized in domestic architecture, J. Morgan Slade was primarily a designer of commercial structures. At the time of his death in 1882, the following comments were made:

> On entering into business on his own account, he soon found himself busily occupied with commission for the construction of mercantile buildings, which many circumstances combined, after his first success, to throw in his way; and this branch of the professional practice claimed nearly all his attention until the time of his death.

"The Death of Mr. J. Morgan Slade, Architect of New York." *American Architect and Building News*, XII (December 9, 1882), 273.

PLATES II.1, 2: *William H. Vanderbilt Residence, corner of Fifth Avenue and 51st Street, New York, N.Y.; 1880–1884; The Herter Brothers; destroyed.*

The Herter Brothers' firm designed the house for three members of the Vanderbilt family: William H., the son of Cornelius Vanderbilt; and William's two daughters, Mrs. E. T. Shepherd and Mrs. W. D. Sloan. Although credited to the Herter Brothers, the house was designed by two members of the firm, Charles B. Atwood (Pl. II.9) and John B. Snook. William H. Vanderbilt died the year following the completion of his residence. Although the house was not ranked in the first twenty, it was included in the 1885 *American Architect* poll.

"The best ten buildings in the United States." *American Architect and Building News*, XVII (June 13, 1885), 283.

Hinckeldeyn, Karl. "William H. Vanderbilt." *Centralblatt der Bauverwaltung*, VI (January 2, 1886), 4–5.

Schuyler, Montgomery. *American Architecture and Other Writing*. Edited by William Jordy and Ralph Coe. Cambridge: The Belknap Press of the Harvard University Press, 1961, 457n, 499–501.

Straham, Edward. *Mr. Vanderbilt's House and Collection*. Boston, New York, and Philadelphia: 1883–1884.

PLATES II.3–5: *Cornelius Vanderbilt Residence, corner of Fifth Avenue and 57th Street, New York, N.Y.; 1879–1882, enlarged to 58th Street 1882–1894; George B. Post; destroyed.*

Montgomery Schuyler, the New York architectural critic, favorably compared the Cornelius Vanderbilt residence to the William K. Vanderbilt house (Pl. II.6) which he considered too ambitious in design and decoration. He concluded that Post's design was more successful, but Hunt's was more interesting. The Cornelius Vanderbilt house was mentioned in the 1885 *American Architect* poll, but it was not ranked among the top twenty.

"The best ten buildings in the United States." *American Architect and Building News*, XVII (June 13, 1885), 283.

Fletcher, Banister F. "American architecture through English spectacles." *Engineering Magazine*, VII (June, 1894), 316.

"House of Cornelius Vanderbilt, Esq., New York, N.Y., Mr. George B. Post, Architect, New York, N.Y." *American Architect and Building News*, XX (May 21, 1881), 247.

Schuyler, Montgomery. *American Architecture and Other Writings*. Edited by William Jordy and Ralph Coe. Cambridge: The Belknap Press of the Harvard University Press, 1961, 493–499.

PLATE II.6: *William K. Vanderbilt Residence, 660 Fifth Avenue, New York, N.Y.; 1879–1881; Richard M. Hunt; destroyed c. 1926.*

Both American and European critics were excited by the design of the William K. Vanderbilt house by Richard Morris Hunt (1827–1895). Montgomery Schuyler considered this mansion to be a summation of French sixteenth-century architecture and rated the sculptural decoration as some of the finest in New York. In 1885, the William K. Vanderbilt house was rated the third best building in the United States in a poll conducted by the *American Architect*; it was the only domestic structure in the top twenty buildings. European critics were more interested in the William K. Vanderbilt house than either of the other two Vanderbilt residences in New York. J. B. Gass included a drawing of it in the 1886 exhibition at the R.I.B.A., and the house was illustrated in numerous American and European periodicals.

"The best ten buildings in the United States." *American Architect and Building News*, XVII (June 13, 1885), 282.

Bing, Samuel. *Artistic America, Tiffany Glass, and Art Nouveau*. Introduction by Robert Koch. Cambridge: The M.I.T. Press, 1970, 62–65.

Bocage, Adolphe. "L'Architecture aux Etats-Unis: La maison moderne et la situation de l'architecte aux Etats-Unis." *L'Architecture*, VII (October 13, 1894), 333.

Cox, Alfred Arthur. "Godwin Bursary Report, 1890." Manuscript. Library of the Royal Institute of British Architects.

"Detail de la façade de l'Hôtel W. K. Vanderbilt à New York." *Le Moniteur des Architectes*, new ser. V (1891), 75.

Gass, John B. "American architecture and architects, with special reference to the late Richard Morris Hunt and Henry Hobson Richardson." *Royal Institute of British Architects, Journal*, ser. 3, III (February 6, 1896), 231.

Schuyler, Montgomery. *American Architecture and Other Writings*. Edited by William Jordy and Ralph Coe. Cambridge: The Belknap Press of the Harvard University Press, 1961, 488.

Van Pelt, John V. *A Monograph of the William K. Vanderbilt House*. New York: 1925.

PLATE II.7: *Governor Samuel J. Tilden Residence, 15 Gramercy Park South, New York, N.Y.; 1872–1874; Calvert Vaux; standing.*

Originally the partner of Andrew Jackson Downing, Calvert Vaux (1824–1892) worked with Frederick Law Olmsted on the plans for Central Park, New York City. The Governor Tilden house and the later Jefferson Market Court House, show Vaux's ability as a designer in the Victorian Gothic mode.

Lamb, Charles R. *The Tilden Mansion—Home of the National Arts Club*. New York: 1952.

Schuyler, Montgomery. *American Architecture and Other Writings*. Edited by William Jordy and Ralph Coe. Cambridge: The Belknap Press of the Harvard University Press, 1961, 479–481.

PLATE II.8: *Ogden O. Goelet Residence, corner of Fifth Avenue and 49th Street, New York, N.Y.; c. 1882; E. H. Kendall; destroyed.*

Edward H. Kendall (1842–1901) also designed the Fifth Avenue residence of Robert Goelet.

*American Architect and Building News*, IX (June 11, 1881), 285.

"A parallel of dormer windows." *American Architect and Building News*, XI (March 4, 1882), 102.

PLATE II.9: *Dr. Stewart Webb Residence, 680 Fifth Avenue; and the H. McKinley Twombley Residence, 684 Fifth Avenue, New York, N.Y.; c. 1885; Charles B. Atwood; destroyed.*

According to Henry F. Withey, Charles B. Atwood worked for the Herter Brothers (Pl. II.1) from 1875 until 1885. Since Atwood alone was credited with the design of the Webb and Stewart houses, it can be assumed that they were designed in 1885 after Atwood left the Herter Brothers' firm. Dr. Stewart Webb, whose house is to the right in the photograph, was the son-in-law of William K. Vanderbilt (Pl. II.6).

Withey, Henry F. and Elsie R. *Biographical Dictionary of American Architects (Deceased)*. Los Angeles: New Age Publishing Company, 1956, 24–25.

PLATE II.10: *John C. Phillips Residence, 229 Berkeley Street, Boston, Mass.; 1877–1879; Peabody and Stearns; destroyed c. 1940.*

Peabody and Stearns' Back Bay house for John C. Phillips is a Boston parallel to the Vanderbilt houses of New York. It was the only Boston house mentioned in the *American Architect's* 1885 poll.

"The best ten buildings in the United States." *American Architect and Building News*, XVII (June 13, 1885), 282.
Holden, Wheaton Arnold. "Robert Swain Peabody of Peabody and Stearns in Boston, the Early Years (1870–1886)." Unpublished Ph.D. dissertation, Boston University, 1969, 87.
"House on Berkeley Street, Boston, Mass." *American Architect and Building News*, XXIII (March 31, 1888), 151.

PLATE II.11: *Detail of the James Converse Residence, 347 Beacon Street, Boston, Mass.; 1884; J. H. Besarick; standing.*

Bunting, Bainbridge. *The House of Boston's Back Bay—An Architectural History 1840–1917*. Cambridge: The Belknap Press of the Harvard University Press, 1967, 227, 407.

PLATE II.12: *Detail of the Oliver Ames Residence, 335 Commonwealth Avenue, Boston, Mass.; 1882; C. Fehmer; standing.*

Oliver Ames was a member of the Ames family that also commissioned H. H. Richardson to design the Town Hall (Pl. I.4) and the gate lodge (Pl. III.38) in North Easton.

*American Architect and Building News*, XV (May 3, 1884), 210.
Bunting, Bainbridge. *Houses of Boston's Back Bay—An Architectural History 1840–1917*. Cambridge: The Belknap Press of the Harvard University Press, 1967, 301.

PLATE II.13: *Augustus Byram Residence, Michigan Avenue near 29th Street, Chicago, Ill.; Burnham and Root.*

*American Architect and Building News*, XI (March 25, 1882), 140.

PLATE II.14: *M. Washburn Residence, 342 Beacon Street, Boston, Mass.; 1880; Allen and Kenway; destroyed.*

*American Architect and Building News*, XIV (July 28, 1883), 42.
Bunting, Bainbridge. *Houses of Boston's Back Bay—An Architectural History 1840–1917*. Cambridge: The Belknap Press of the Harvard University Press, 1967, 223–225, 408.

PLATE II.16: *Private Residence, Chicago, Ill.; Wheelock and Clay.*

Otis Leonard Wheelock (1816–1886) and William W. Clay are the most widely illustrated Chicago architects in *L'Architecture Américaine*. In a biographical sketch of William Clay, Henry F. Withey commented:

He [Clay] was better known, however, for his residence work which comprised many homes for wealthy clients on Prairie Avenue, and hundreds of other houses both large and small, in the city. It may also be of interest to recall that he was the first architect in Chicago to make use of encaustic tile as exterior decoration of private homes.

Withey, Henry F. and Elsie R. *Biographical Dictionary of American Architects (Deceased)*. Los Angeles: New Age Publishing Company, 1956, 125.

PLATE II.19: *John E. Bell Residence, 306 McMillan Street, Cincinnati, O.; 1881–1882; Samuel Hannaford; destroyed.*

Samuel Hannaford (1835–1910) used blue sandstone and Ohio River sandstone, popular building materials in Cincinnati at that time, for the construction of the Bell house. At the time of construction, the house was actually in a suburb of Cincinnati—Walnut Hills—that was later swallowed by the city's growth.

"House for John E. Bell, Esq., Walnut Hills, Cincinnati, O., Mr. Samuel Hannaford, Architect, Cincinnati, O." *American Architect and Building News*, XI (February 25, 1882), 90.

PLATE II.21: *Simon J. Murphy Residence, corner of Woodward and Putnam streets, Detroit, Mich.; William Scott and Company; destroyed.*

Designed for a Detroit lumber baron, the Simon J. Murphy house was not published in *Inland Architect* until 1887, but it would have had to have been completed by 1885 to be included in *L'Architecture Américaine*.

Ferry, W. Hawkins. *The Buildings of Detroit—A History*. Detroit: Wayne State University Press, 1968, 80, 92.

PLATE II.23: *Private Residence, 28 West 54th Street, New York, N.Y.; 1881; R. H. Robertson.*

*A History of Real Estate, Building and Architecture in New York City During the Last Quarter of a Century*. New York: 1898, 634.

PLATE II.25: *Private Residence, 135 Marlborough Street, Boston, Mass.; 1880; Cabot and Chandler; standing.*

Bunting, Bainbridge. *Houses of Boston's Back Bay—An Architectural History 1840–1917*. Cambridge: The Belknap Press of the Harvard University Press, 1967, 232.

PLATE II.26: *H. Tuttle Residence, 321 Commonwealth Avenue; and the Horace Billings Residence, 323 Commonwealth Avenue, Boston Mass.; 1879; Kirby and Lewis; standing.*

The half of a house at the right of the photograph was also designed by Kirby and Lewis in 1878 for Asa Caton.

*American Architect and Building News*, IV (November 23, 1878), 172.
*American Architect and Building News*, VIII (November 27, 1880), 258.
Bunting, Bainbridge. *Houses of Boston's Back Bay—An Architectural History 1840–1917*. Cambridge: The Belknap Press of the Harvard University Press, 1967, 428.

PLATE II.27: *Residences for Asa Caton, 337, 339, and 341 Commonwealth Avenue, Boston, Mass.; 1880; Kirby and Lewis; standing.*

Bunting, Bainbridge. *Houses of Boston's Back Bay—An Architectural History 1840–1917*. Cambridge: The Belknap Press of the Harvard University Press, 1967, 428.

PLATE II.29: *"The Berkshires," northwest corner of Madison Avenue and 52nd Street, New York, N.Y.; c. 1883–1884; Carl Pfeifer; destroyed.*

Carl Pfeifer (1838–1888) was both the architect and a client for this apartment building. He organized eight shareholders who advanced the money for construction and then became one of the corporate owners and occupants of the building. "The Berkshires" contained only seventeen apartments, each including ten rooms and extra service area. The building was completely heated by steam and contained two elevators and an incinerator in the basement.

"'The Berkshires,' New York, N.Y., Mr. Carl Pfeifer, architect, New York, N.Y." *American Architect and Building News*, XIV (August 4, 1883), 53–54.

Gale, A. J. "English impressions of American architecture." *Builder*, XLIX (December 19, 1885), 854.

PLATE II.30: *Vestibule of the Joseph H. White Residence, Fisher Hill, Brookline, Mass.; 1880–1881; Peabody and Stearns; standing.*

The vestibule from the White house (Pl. III.17) was closely described in Appleton's *Artistic Houses . . .*, in 1883:

Standing with our backs against the piazza door . . . we see a wide oaken stairway, of easy ascent, and at its right an entrance into the billard-room. . . . The walls are wainscoted to a height of five feet, and then tinted in Indian-red, which, together with tints of gold, brown, and gray, appear again in the panels of the heavily beamed ceiling. . . . there is a large center-table, eight feet long by five feet wide, on which, in addition to a variety of choice books, appear vases filled with fuchsias, English primroses, and umbrella ferns.

*Artistic Houses, being a series of interior views of a number of the most beautiful and celebrated homes in the United States, with a description of the art treasures contained therein.* New York: D. Appleton, 1883–1884, 139–140.

PLATE II.33: *Dining-room Buffet of a Private Residence, Cleveland, O.; L. T. Schofield.*

Levi T. Scofield (1842–1917), the designer of this sculptural dining-room buffet, was most noted for his public monuments. After returning from the Civil War, Scofield spent seven years as the designer, sculptor, and architect of the Soldiers' and Sailors' Monument in Public Square, Cleveland.

Withey, Henry F. and Elsie R. *Biographical Dictionary of American Architects (Deceased).* Los Angeles: New Age Publishing Company, 1956, 543–544.

PLATES II.34, 35, 39: *Three Rooms for the Samuel M. Nickerson Residence, 40 East Erie Street, Chicago, Ill.; 1883; Burling and Whitehouse (architects), and A. Fiedler (decorator); standing.*

The dining room (Pl. II.34), smoking room (Pl. II.35), and bedroom (Pl. II.39) are all from the S. M. Nickerson residence. These rooms were closely described in *Artistic Houses* which noted the Flemish Renaissance style of the dining room, the high wainscoting of the smoking room with shelves for "collected *bric-à-brac*," and the general finish of the bedrooms with high wainscoting and a canvas ceiling divided by wooden or brass moldings.

*American Architect and Building News*, XX (July 17, 1886), 30.

*Artistic Houses, being a series of interior views of a number of the most beautiful and celebrated homes in the United States, with a description of the art treasures contained therein.* New York: D. Appleton, 1883–1884, 50–51.

Coles, William A., ed. *Architecture and Society—Selected Essays by Henry Van Brunt.* Cambridge: The Belknap Press of the Harvard University Press, 1969, 194.

PLATE II.36: *Fireplace of the Oakes Ames Memorial Library, North Easton, Mass.; 1877; H. H. Richardson; standing.*

The mantel from the North Easton Library (see Note I.4) shows the strong influence of the English Pre-Raphaelites. Henry-Russell Hitchcock believes that the mantel was designed by Stanford White, then a draughtsman in Richardson's office. Except for a decorative mantel in Austin Hall (Pl. I.9) this fireplace design is a unique example in Richardson's work.

Hitchcock, Henry-Russell. *The Architecture of H. H. Richardson and His Times.* Revised ed. Cambridge: The M.I.T. Press, 1961, 186–187.

PLATE II.37: *Fireplace of the Ladies' Parlor, the R. H. White Store, 30 Bedford Street, Boston, Mass.; 1881; Peabody and Stearns; standing.*

Located in the addition to the R. H. White Store (Pl. I.30) by Peabody and Stearns, this mantel was the focal point of a large room. The following description appeared in Appleton's *Artistic Houses*:

The walls are of plaster, painted many times in a low, deep tint, suggestive of old gold; the arch inclosing the clock is of glass mosaic; and the immense fire-place has a facing of Victoria marble, a lining and hearth of glazed tile, and a back of iron.

*American Architect and Building News*, XVI (September 6, 1884), 117.

*Artistic Houses, being a series of interior views of a number of the most beautiful and celebrated homes in the United States, with a description of the art treasures contained therein.* New York: D. Appelton, 1883–1884, 125.

Holden, Wheaton Arnold. "Robert Swain Peabody of Peabody and Stearns in Boston—The Early Years (1870–1886)." Unpublished Ph.D. dissertation, Boston University 1969, 117.

Schuyler, Montgomery. "The Romanesque Revival in America." *Architectural Record*, I (1892), 174–175.

PLATE II.38: *Music Room and Conservatory of a Private Residence, New York, N.Y.; H. J. Schwartzmann and Company.*

Herman J. Schwartzmann (1843–1891) was the Architect-in-Chief of the 1876 Centennial in Philadelphia where he designed Memorial Hall and Horticultural Hall. Following the close of the Exhibition, he moved to New York City and established a partnership with Alfred Buchman which lasted until 1890. Perhaps Schwartzmann received the commission for this conservatory because of the reputation of his Horticultural Hall.

Withey, Henry F. and Elsie R. *Biographical Dictionary of American Architects (Deceased).* Los Angeles: New Age Publishing Company, 1956, 542–543.

PLATE III.1: *Cornelius Kingsland Garrison Villa, northeast corner of Ocean and Park avenues, Elberon, N.J.; 1881–1882; C. K. Garrison; destroyed c. 1940.*

Cornelius Kingsland Garrison (1809–1885) was a capitalist, railroad builder, architect and engineer who purchased land in Elberon in 1881 and designed his own seaside mansion. Painted bright yellow with green trim, the house was known as "The House of Many Gables" and "Aladdin's Palace." After Garrison's death in 1885, the house was leased to Mayor Fitler of Philadelphia and sold to Solomon R. Guggenheim in 1899.

PLATE III.2: *Charles G. Francklyn Residence, Elberon, N.J.; c. 1876; McKim, Mead and White; destroyed.*

A drawing by Charles McKim of this cottage was published in 1876, presumably close to the date of construction. The following year, Francklyn employed McKim, Mead and White to design the Elberon Hotel which was constructed on Ocean Avenue, near the Kinney Residence (Pl. III.3).

"Cottage for Charles G. Francklyn, Esq., Long Branch, N.J." *The New York Sketch-Book of Architecture*, III (December, 1876), plate XLVII.

PLATE III.3: *Thomas T. Kinney Residence, southwest corner of Ocean and Lincoln avenues, Elberon, N.J.; 1881; V. C. Taylor; destroyed.*

Thomas T. Kinney, editor of the Newark *Daily Advertiser*, purchased a lot in Elberon in 1879 and, two years later, employed Van Campen Taylor, also of Newark, to design a cottage. Unlike many of the Elberon houses that were built on piers, the Thomas T. Kinney house was constructed on a full basement. The interior of both the Kinney house and the Garrison villa (Pl. III.1) were finished with California redwood.

Sheldon, George W. *Artistic Country Seats; types of recent American villa and cottage architecture; with instances of country clubhouses* . . . New York: D. Appleton and Co., 1886, V, 125–127.

PLATE III.4: *"Château-Nooga," the C. C. Baldwin Residence, Bellevue Avenue, Newport, R.I.; 1880–1881; G. B. Post; standing.*

Downing, Antoinette and Scully, Vincent J., Jr. *The Architectural Heritage of Newport, Rhode Island 1640–1915.* 2nd ed. New York: Clarkson N. Potter, 1967, 158–159.

PLATE III.5: *"Vinland," the Catherine Lorillard Wolfe Residence, Newport, R.I.; 1882–1884; Peabody and Stearns; standing.*

Considered "one of the most comfortable, commodious, and beautiful country seats in the world" by George W. Sheldon, "Vinland" was completely furnished and decorated by Richard Codman of Boston. The gate lodge (Pl. III.40) to "Vinland" was also designed by Peabody and Stearns.

Holden, Wheaton Arnold. "Robert Swain Peabody of Peabody and Stearns in Boston—The Early Years (1870–1886)." Unpublished Ph.D. dissertation, Boston University, 1969, 141–142.
Schuyler, Montgomery. "The Romanesque Revival in America." *Architectural Record*, I (1892), 195.

PLATE III.6: *"Chatwold," the Mrs. G. B. Bowler Residence, Bar Harbor, Me.; Rotch and Tilden; destroyed.*

Since Arthur Rotch (1850–1894) and George Thomas Tilden (1845–1919) did not form their partnership until 1881, this house was constructed sometime between 1881 and 1885. At Bar Harbor and Newport, resort houses were being built to provide all the comforts of urban residences. In discussing "Chatwold," George Sheldon emphasized this idea of permanence by quoting a long passage from Ruskin's *Seven Lamps of Architecture* concerning sturdy construction that will last for generations. "Chatwold," in part a wooden structure, was destroyed by fire in the early twentieth century.

"Amerikanische Landhäuser." *Deutsche Bauzeitung*, XXI (September 10, 1887), 433.
"'Chatwold,' Mt. Desert, Me., Rotch and Tilden, Architects." *American Architect and Building News*, XIII (March 3, 1883), 103.
Sheldon, George W. *Artistic Country Seats; types of recent American villa and cottage architecture; with instances of country clubhouses* . . . New York: D. Appleton and Co.,1886, II, 135.

PLATE III.9: *Private Residence, Orange, N.J.; A. H. Dodd.*

"Maison de campagne près de New York." *La Semaine des Constructeurs*, ser. 2, II (February 18, 1888), 401.

PLATE III.11: *Henry C. Pedder Residence, Llewellyn Park, Orange, N.J.; H. H. Holly; standing.*

Henry Hudson Holly (1834–1892), author of a book on country seats (1863), designed this large frame house in Llewellyn Park. Although built by Henry Pedder, the house was later purchased and named "Glenmont" by Thomas A. Edison who maintained his laboratories nearby. Following a common practice of the period, each of the main rooms of the house was finished in a different wood.

"House for Mr. Henry C. Pedder, Llewellyn Park, Orange, N.J., Mr. H. H. Holly, Architect, New York, N.Y." *American Architect and Building News*, X (August 27, 1881), 98.
Whittemore, Henry. *The Founders and Builders of the Oranges* . . . Newark: L. J. Hardham, 1896, 334.

PLATE III.12: *Antoinette Phelps Residence, 276 Washington Street, Hartford, Ct.; c. 1880; George Keller; standing.*

George W. Keller (1842–1935), a prolific Connecticut architect, probably designed this house in 1880 for Miss Antoinette Phelps who lived in a house on this site from that date until 1909. Keller was also interested in providing good design for families of middle and lower incomes.

PLATE III.13: *Dr. G. Pierrepont Davis Residence, 30 Woodland Street, Hartford, Ct.; 1881; F. C. Withers; destroyed.*

*American Architect and Building News*, IX (July 18, 1881), 296.

PLATE III.14: *Franklin Chamberlin Residence, 77 Forest Street, Hartford, Ct.; 1881–1884; Kimball and Wisedell; standing.*

In 1869, Francis Kimball was sent to Hartford as the representative of the Louis P. Rogers firm of Boston, in the construction of buildings for the Charter Oak Life Insurance Company and the Connecticut Mutual Life Insurance Company. He was subsequently employed to supervise William Burges' plans for the new campus of Trinity College in Hartford. In 1879, Kimball moved to New York City and formed a partnership with Thomas Wisedell (see Note I.12). Kimball's Hartford connections brought him this commission for a house for Franklin Chamberlin, a prominent Hartford lawyer. Today, the Chamberlin house is the headquarters for the Stowe-Day Foundation which maintains a research library and administers the Harriet Beecher Stowe house, its immediate neighbor. Drawings by Kimball and Wisedell for the Chamberlin house are held in the Foundation library.

Schuyler, Montgomery. "The works of Francis H. Kimball and Kimball & Thompson." *Architectural Record*, VII (April–June, 1898), 479–485.

PLATE III.16: *Edward Stanwood Residence, 76 High Street, Brookline, Mass.; 1880; C. S. Luce; standing.*

*American Architect and Building News*, VII (February 28, 1880), 82.

PLATE III.17: *Joseph H. White Residence, Fisher Hill, Brookline, Mass.; 1880–1881; Peabody and Stearns; standing.*

In addition to this residence and its stable and gardener's house, Peabody and Stearns also designed two Boston stores for Joseph H. White (Pls. I.30, II.30, 37). Frederick Law Olmsted landscaped the grounds of the White house.

PLATE III.21: *John Greenough Residence, 15 Greenough Avenue, Jamaica Plain, Mass.; 1880; W. R. Emerson; standing.*

In January, 1880, the *American Architect* published a drawing of two houses by William Ralph Emerson for J. Greenough. Two months later, the magazine announced that Emerson's houses for Greenough would be built that summer. Although the drawings for the Greenough houses and this photograph (Pl. III.21) are completely different, this is probably the house built for Greenough in the summer of 1880.

*American Architect and Building News*, VII (January 31, 1880), 37.
*American Architect and Building News*, VII (March 20, 1880), 124.
Hamlin, Talbot. *American Spirit in Architecture*. Vol. XIII of *The Pageant of America*. New Haven: Yale University Press, 1952, 167.
Scully, Vincent J., Jr. *The Shingle Style and the Stick Style—Architectural Theory and Design from Richardson to the Origins of Wright*. Revised edition. New Haven: Yale University Press, 1971, 85.

PLATE III.22: *Private Residence, 101 Forest Hills Street, Jamaica Plain, Mass.; W. R. Emerson; standing.*

Emerson, who had a penchant for the Colonial revival style, designed many houses similar to this one in Jamaica Plain. It was probably built for Elizabeth Q. Huntington, who was its owner in 1890.

PLATES III.25–27: *Private Residences, Buffalo, N.Y.; J. L. Silsbee.*

An early teacher of Frank Lloyd Wright, James Lyman Silsbee (1845–1913) worked on the interior of the Potter Palmer house in Chicago. Plates III.25, 26 are two views of the same house by Silsbee. Plate III.27 was published in the *American Architect* without any information about client, date, or location. These houses were probably designed before Silsbee left Syracuse for Chicago in 1884.

"House at Buffalo, N.Y., Mr. J. L. Silsbee, Architect, Syracuse, N.Y." *American Architect and Building News*, XV (April 12, 1884), 174.
Scully, Vincent J. Jr. *The Shingle Style and the Stick Style—Architectural Theory and Design from Richardson to the Origins of Wright*. New Haven: Yale University Press, 1971, 158–159.

PLATE III.28: *Private Residence, Chicago, Ill.; Cobb and Frost.*

Having both begun their careers with Peabody and Stearns, Henry Ives Cobb (1859–1931) and Charles Sumner Frost (1856–1931) moved to Chicago in 1882 when Cobb won the design competition for the Chicago Union League Club. Thus, it is logical to assume that this Cobb and Frost house was constructed sometime between 1882 and 1885. Henry F. Withey summarized their work as follows:

> In the field of residential work, Cobb and Frost won wide recognition following the completion of the Potter Palmer mansion at the corner of Lake Shore Drive and Banks Street, for which a permit was taken out for $90,000. Other residences of note designed by the firm included the Dr. Gill home on Drexel Boulevard and the Cass house, Chicago.

Withey, Henry F. and Elsie R. *Biographical Dictionary of American Architects (Deceased)*. Los Angeles: New Age Publishing Company, 1956, 129.

PLATE III.30: *Elbridge Torrey Residence, corner of Mellville Avenue and Washington Street, Dorchester, Mass.; 1880; Cabot and Chandler.*

"Dwelling for Mr. E. Torrey, Esq., Dorchester, Mass., Messrs. Cabot and Chandler, Architects, Boston." *American Architect and Building News*, VII (April 3, 1880), 127.

PLATE III.34: *J. M. Wayne Neff Residence, southwest corner of Oak Street and Reading Road, Cincinnati, O.; 1881; Bruce Price; destroyed.*

Bruce Price (1843–1903) began his career in Baltimore, working for E. T. Baldwin (Pl. I.19), moved later to Wilkes-Barre, Pennsylvania, and then to New York City. The Neff house shows a combination of French and English influences on both the exterior and the interior. The tower is modeled on a French dovecote although the half-timbered decoration is strongly English. The parlor was furnished in a Louis Quatorze style, while the library and dining room were finished in cherry and decorated in a more English fashion.

"House for J. M. Wayne Neff, Esq., Cincinnati, O., Mr. Bruce Price, Architect, New York, N.Y." *American Architect and Building News*, XI (February 4, 1882), 55.
Sheldon, George W. *Artistic Country Seats; types of recent American villa and cottage architecture: with instances of country clubhouses* . . . New York: D. Appleton, 1886, IV, 75–76.

PLATE III.35: *M. D. Wells Residence, southeast corner of Michigan Avenue and 26th Street, Chicago, Ill.; Wheelock and Clay.*

*Inland Architect and News Record*, III (March, 1884), 23.

PLATE III.37: *Private Residences, Groveland Avenue, Chicago, Ill.; Wheelock and Clay.*

The house at the left in the photograph, 3228 Groveland Avenue, was definitely by Wheelock and Clay. There is no information presently available on the house at the right.

*Inland Architect and News Record*, VI (November, 1885), 51.

PLATES III.38, 39: *F. L. Ames Gate Lodge, North Easton Mass.; 1880; H. H. Richardson; standing.*

Richardson designed this gate lodge for his close friend, F. L. Ames, a member of the family that gave him so many commissions (Pl. I.4). The gate lodge (Pl. III.39) included a potting shed and orangery, to the left of the portal, and living quarters to the right. The grounds of the F. L. Ames estate were landscaped by Frederick Law Olmsted.

"Two American lodges." *Builder*, LVI (January 5, 1889), 12. Hitchcock, Henry-Russell. *The Architecture of H. H. Richardson and His Times.* Cambridge: The M.I.T. Press, 1961, 202–204.

PLATE III.40: *Catherine Lorillard Wolfe Gate Lodge, "Vinland," Newport, R.I.; 1882–1884; Peabody and Stearns; standing.*

In addition to the gate lodge for "Vinland" (Pl. III.5), Peabody and Stearns also designed a henhouse and gardener's cottage as dependencies to this estate.

Holden, Wheaton Arnold. "The Peabody Touch: Peabody and Stearns of Boston, 1870–1917." *Journal of the Society of Architectural Historians*, XXXII (May, 1973), 121–122.